THE MOUSE THAT ROARED ON SATURDAY: BRIAN HENNINGER AT THE 1995 MASTERS

BY: BRIAN H. HENNINGER
With: Brent Summers

"Let Superman Fly"

Golf-in-Oregon Publications
Contact: Brent Summers
(503) 968-9000

Printed By Adibooks.com

USA

ISBN 0-9767424-4-6

Identification of Photographs and Photography Credits

Cover: Brian Henninger at the par-3 sixteenth at Augusta National. Photo by Blake Madden, © The Augusta Chronicle and re-printed with permission.

Back: Brian Henninger on the tee at the ninth hole, Augusta National Par-3 Course. Photo by my friend Gene Tupper, re-printed with permission.

Inside black and white photographs of my family and Gary and Barbara Pasquinelli were taken by family and friends at the 1995 Masters. Cathy and I stopped for a photo with Jack and Barbara Nicklaus at the New Orleans, Louisiana Tour stop. David Whitt swinging away at the Fireside Chat. My mentors, Peter Jacobsen and Dick Helmstetter at the Fireside Chat. The ocean from Bandon Dunes and Cathy's championship trophy oil painting on the brochure cover for the 2001 Fireside Chat. Dick Helmstetter with me and Team Callaway at the 2001 Fireside Chat in Sunriver, Oregon. Fireside Chat photos by Scott Bisch. All re-printed here with permission.

DEDICATIONS

This book is lovingly dedicated to the mother of Carlin, Hunter and Mia:

Catherine Henninger

You inspire me every day.

This book is also dedicated to:

Underdogs Everywhere

When you look up the word "underdog" in the Microsoft Word Thesaurus, the words "small fry," "runner up," and "little guy" appear on the screen. This book is also dedicated to underdogs everywhere, other little guys like me who, in the words of Chief Dan George's character in The Outlaw Jose Wales, "endeavor to persevere."

THE MOUSE THAT ROARED ON SATURDAY: BRIAN HENNINGER AT THE 1995 MASTERS

TABLE OF CONTENTS   Page

THE MOUSE THAT ROARED ON SATURDAY; BRIAN HENNINGER AT THE 1995 MASTERS

Prologue

"After Saturday's round, it was over for me—it felt as though I had already won the golf tournament."

Brian Henninger, March 14, 2005

I was sitting in a Board meeting for my charitable foundation on March 8, 2005, when one of the other board members reminded me that the ten-year anniversary of my success at the 1995 Masters was only a month away. He also reminded me that I had threatened many times to write a book about that experience and its impact on my life and my golf game. He suggested that if I was ever going to make good on that threat, it would be good to get busy. Immediately. He told me I needed to put the book together for publication by April 1, 2005 in order to capitalize on the ten-year anniversary of that special time.

There are three things for which I am generally known as a professional golfer. These are the subjects that people I meet want to talk about as I play in Pro-Ams and go about my business around the Country. By far the largest number of people remember the magic of my third round of the Masters Tournament at Augusta National on Saturday, April 8, 1995. Even though I did not win the tournament, that day remains the high point of my career. The next most-remembered career moment has to be the 4-iron I hit on the seventy-second hole at the 1994 Bell-South Classic, together with the eight foot putt I made for eagle as I tried, in vain, to catch John Daly from behind. Third, a great number of people have read about my trials and tribulations on Tour and at Qualifying School in John Feinstein's A Good Walk Spoiled (Little, Brown 1995). My friends and followers in the Pacific Northwest will also note that in 2002, I won the final staging of Peter Jacobsen's Fred Meyer Challenge with Scott McCarron, my best friend on Tour. My friends on Tour would also point out a fifth accomplishment, my second Tour victory at the 1999 Southern Farm Bureau Classic.

To some degree, this book is about all of the significant events and people that have made my life so special as a PGA Tour player. But the special week I spent in April of 1995 on the hallowed ground of Augusta National Golf Club remains the driving force for the effort I have put in here to try and make sense of it all.

CHAPTER ONE

"On Brink of History, Henninger Synonymous With Anonymous."

--Thomas Boswell, The Washington Post 4-9-95

"Which man would it be? Young Brian Henninger, another co-leader, whose play on Saturday had been pure magic?"

Masters 1995, Augusta National Golf Club, p. 50 (1995)

Early in the telecast of Saturday's action, Jim Nantz, the exceptionally talented CBS golf anchor, broke in to update the leader board with the following:

> "We have another name now, joining Strange and Crenshaw, it's a first time Masters player, Brian Henninger, out of USC. Some gutsy little player he is, who last year was a runner up at Atlanta and won down at Hattiesburg, Mississippi. And, Henninger at one point on Thursday, was 4 over for the tournament. He's 12 under since that time, since the fifth hole on Thursday."

I was playing the difficult eleventh hole at the time. I had hit one of very few bad tee shots on the day and missed the green with my recovery out of those most famous of Georgia woods. I had to make a great chip to save par. Verne Lundquist had the call:

> "And here is Brian Henninger, Jim, this is his third shot. In the woods off the tee to the right, pitched out, and what a wonderful little chip shot. For this 31-year old, there is a huge scoreboard just to his left. He's playing his first Masters. What a thrill it must be for him to look over and see his name listed among the quartet at the top. Brian Henninger, and a chance to save par here."

I made the putt and saved par. But I never looked at the leader board. In fact, I had no idea all day long where I was in relation to the field. For me, and for most Tour players, that is extremely rare. More than 98 percent of the time, we know exactly where we are in relation to the field, especially if we are leading the golf tournament. There were a lot of strange things about that Saturday though, and this was one of them. I was just out playing a relaxed round of golf with Davis Love, III.

It was on to the dangerous par 3 twelfth hole and more Verne Lundquist:

> "And back on the tee at the twelfth. Home town of Lake Oswego, Oregon. Won at the Deposit Guaranty last year, but really attracted our attention with a second place finish to John Daly at Atlanta when he played with such courage coming down the stretch. First appearance in the Masters. He has parred this hole the first two days. Back-left."

I missed the green to a safe spot, back-left. I hit a fair chip shot to about six feet and missed the putt for my second bogey of the round. Now, at the par 5 thirteenth, the birdie holes and the fireworks began. Tom Weiskopf had the call:

> "Brian Henninger, 190, with 185 to carry the water. He's pulled this shot a bit. Will it stay? Not quite. Not a difficult shot from there, however. That's the place you want to miss it if you are going to go at this green. . . . . And that was a three foot effort. Brian Henninger's birdie moves him to eight under at this moment. A beautiful little pitch he played from behind the green. Excellent shot."

I really did not pull the approach shot at all. I hit it right where I was looking and the ball failed to fade back toward the pin. Still, it was a very well executed shot and with a little cut, I would have been very close for eagle. The ball landed hard and rolled off the back of the green in testimony to how fast Augusta National was playing. I was very proud of my chip shot to three feet. In looking back at the tape of the telecast, at this point I was sorry CBS had not been able to show more of my great chips, like the ones at eleven and thirteen. I walked off the thirteenth green, with my sixteenth birdie in forty-four holes. Little did I know, one of my chip shots soon to come would cause quite a stir and garner an extraordinary amount of air time. Jim Nantz summarized the leader board:

> "Ben Crenshaw by one over Curtis Strange who went out early and shot 65 today. Steve Elkington at

eight under. Brian Henninger, who did not even join a high school golf team until his senior year in high school back in Lake Oswego, Oregon. He took up the game late. Walked on to the golf team at Southern Cal. He qualified by winning his first tour event last year. He's only one back in his first Masters. And Jay Haas with a nice move after some early damage. Then the names like Norman and Couples lurk . . . ."

I hit a great second shot to about twelve feet at fourteen. I hit the birdie putt a little too hard as I was trying to make it. We often tell amateur players that trying to make birdie putts, or even par putts of any length will lead to a three-putt. The advice we give is to "lag and let the hole get in the way." I was having none of that on the back-nine at Augusta as I stood over the birdie putt at fourteen. The putt was very make-able and I just hit it too hard for as much break as I borrowed on the high side of the hole. The announcer, Tom Weiskopf, thought I was nervous:

> "Brian Henninger to tie for the lead. Two inches outside right lip. Just too strong. Wouldn't take the break. Oh, how hard speed is when the nerves are twitching."

I assure you, for reasons that have escaped me for the past ten years, I was never nervous at all on that Saturday at Augusta. The sole exception may have been when I heard my name announced on the first tee. I say that today, because that always makes me nervous, but in a good way. The announcement of my name kick-starts the nervous anticipation of great things to come in the golf round. I take a deep breath, go through my pre-shot routine and then (hopefully) bust it down the middle on number one. Then, the nerves are gone. At least until the least controllable aspect of my game, my brain, takes over and lets the nerves back in.

I think I have figured out some of the answers to why I was not nervous that Saturday, but I cannot be certain. One reason, for sure, was the manner in which I was treated by Davis Love, III, my playing partner. Davis knew I did not have a great deal of experience in a situation like this, and he was so thoughtful and complimentary about my experience that he had a huge calming influence on me. As I said before, it was like the two of us were just out for a fun day on the golf course. Never mind the television cameras and the colorful multitudes of appreciative fans among the rich and splendid backdrop that is Augusta National. Anyway, let's move up to fifteen and the one and only Ben Wright:

> "And young Brian Hennninger who was a Nike Tour player in 1992, his first Masters. That's a very good play *indeed* by Henninger, a lovely little chip. . . Brian Henninger with his birdie opportunity. To get to nine under for this youngster who has missed four cuts in 1995. Just one highly respectable finish--he tied for twelfth in Hawaii. But this is a colossal performance in a first Masters Tournament."

I hit another great chip shot to about two feet and made the putt for birdie. While over the ball prior to the chip, however, I touched the ball with my wedge. The CBS director in the mobile studio had directed a close-up of my ball. The image of my club touching the ball set off a firestorm of telephone calls to CBS and Augusta National, inquiring whether a violation of the rules had occurred. Jim Nantz, who was so very kind to me during this telecast and many others, cleared up the controversy at the beginning of Sunday's telecast:

> "We want to clear the air concerning an incident yesterday at the fifteenth involving Brian Henninger. Hundreds of callers from around the World spotted this. As he addressed his third shot the ball wobbled, fluttered if you will. But Rule 18 states that: 'A ball is deemed to have moved if it leaves its position and comes to rest in any other place.' Well, clearly, as we played it back a couple of times, as you saw, by definition, the ball never changed position."

After the round, when I was questioned by tournament officials about the chip shot on fifteen, I had no idea what they were talking about. I was able to answer to the best of my knowledge, in fact to my only knowledge that the ball never moved on any of my shots that day. I was never called to the CBS truck to review the tape, so the matter must have been resolved shortly after I was first approached by the officials.

The good news at fifteen was that I made yet another birdie. We headed to the spectacular par 3 sixteenth that was playing a short 148 yards. I hit a solid 8-iron that carried just a little too far, causing my ball to roll down the steep green more than 40 feet from the hole. Again, the irrepressible Ben Wright had the call:

> "Brian Henninger's tee shot on its way on this 165 yard terror stretch. Oh, that will go a long way down into the bottom. And, Cory Pavin and Lee Janzen have both just three-putted from that position to fall back, both of them, to four under par. So, Brian Henninger has got a severe test."

The cameras then cut to 1992 Masters Champion Fred Couples walking up the eighteenth fairway but quickly returned to the tee box at sixteen for Davis Love's tee shot. Once more, the erudite Mr. Wright, as Davis hit the ball to a foot from the hole:

> "Don't go away now. Beautiful. Fantastic shot by Davis, who is at six under par, about to go seven under. What a story that would be, he qualified just a week before. A monstrous roar!"

Davis walked up to mark his ball to a raucous standing ovation. I went about my business of figuring out how to get my first putt close. The severe break was readable and very apparent. The difficulty was gauging the speed, going up the hill, with the ball falling away to the right towards the hole as it crested the hill. All I was thinking about was avoiding a three-putt and giving back one of the birdies I had worked so hard for on thirteen and fifteen. Mr. Ben Wright:

> "And now, to the sixteenth and Brian Henninger, trying to get down in two. . . . And the caddy's head obscures the fact that he made an absolutely improbable putt to tie the leader Ben Crenshaw at ten under par. What a romantic story. Thirty-one years

old from Lake Oswego, Oregon. And now, Davis Love for a cinch. At seven under, now three behind his fellow competitor, Brian Henninger."

Davis tapped in for his two from a foot away. He then raised his arms to the crowd and shrugged his shoulders, giving me the stage. He made a big deal about my putt, even though he had made a terrific shot to almost hole out. I have no recollection of pumping my fist or making the face that CBS replayed several times in recapping the third round of play. It was pure involuntary reaction out of total shock. A photograph of that moment appeared on the front page of the Augusta Chronicle, which hangs on the wall of my office. That moment will always be the epitome of my special day at the Masters. I like to think the moment was special to the wonderful fans that were there to share the moment, and to the members of Augusta National. Indeed, the moment was described in Augusta National's official publication of the 1995 Maters Tournament as follows:

> "The day's biggest story, however, was 31-year-old Brian Henninger, an unheralded Oregonian who didn't start playing golf until he was a senior in high school. Henninger had begun this Masters by bogeying four of his first five holes, but had fought back over the next 49, registering 18 birdies (the most in the field) against only four more bogeys. On Saturday afternoon, just as he might have been expected to crack, the Masters first-timer made his move with birdies at 13, 15, and 16, the last of them coming on a dramatic side winding uphill putt."

“’When I made that putt, I remembered Jack Nicklaus [and the birdie putt he made at 16 on Sunday in 1975],’ said Henninger. ‘I could feel his presence down there.’”

Masters 1995, Augusta National Golf Club, p. 40 (1995). That publication, in Masters-green hardcover, is the golf publication I cherish the most. It is also probably my most cherished memento of any golf tournament I have ever played in. I had always watched Jack Nicklaus as I was growing up, especially at the Masters. Because he was so successful, I followed Mr. Nicklaus’s career fairly close, even though I never played any competitive golf until I was a senior in high school. As I was having success at Augusta over the first three rounds, and on Saturday in particular, I drew on the images of Jack Nicklaus that were stuck in my mind from those years of watching him on television. To this day, I believe those images helped me be creative with some of my shots and putts, something you have to do to be successful at Augusta.

Next it was on to the seventeenth. I was really swinging well and had hit the driver perfect all day. I caught another one absolutely flush, and I was fortunate to have one of my all-time favorite players and announcers, Bobby Clampett, calling the action at seventeen:

“And, Brian Henninger off the tee. Perfectly placed. The right side of the fairway. This little guy can pound it out there. . . . At five-eight, Brian Henninger. A hundred and fifteen yards. That’s five yards past where Freddy drove it. For a guy five-eight, one fifty-five, that's killing it."

Bobby, right about everything else, was heavy by fifteen pounds. At the 1995 Masters, I was still five feet-eight inches tall, but I weighed 140 pounds dripping wet. Remember, guys my size are not supposed to be able to play well at Augusta.

At that point in the telecast, Jim Nantz and the legendary U.S. Open champion and long-time CBS color announcer Ken Venturi, paid homage to my effort to catch John Daly from behind at Atlanta the year before:

> JN: "Well, take note here folks, of this gutsy little five foot-eight ball of fire named Brian Henninger. Tied for the lead in his first Masters at ten under with Ben Crenshaw. Kenny, you'll never forget the 4-iron at Atlanta last year. One of the most clutch shots of the year."
>
> KV: "That showed how long he was."

And, for the first time in the telecast, as Jim Nantz began that conversation with Ken Venturi, the television leader board showed my name at the very top. The next images of me showed the solid four foot putt I had to make to save par on seventeen after hitting a poor birdie putt from the fringe. As the putt went in, Bobby Clampett reminded the audience of my poor start on Thursday:

> "Boy, for a man who started four over after his first five holes in the Masters, I would have to say the nerves have settled."

Finally someone, Bobby, had it exactly right. I was perfectly calm as further evidenced by the eight footer I had to make at eighteen to hold a share of the third round lead with Ben Crenshaw. As I stepped to the tee at eighteen, Jim Nantz told another story:

> "Brian Henninger on the tee here. I'll tell you what kind of battler he is, Kenny, he was a very good junior tennis player. He competed all across the United States and then took up the game [of golf] his senior year of high school and won the state high school championship out of the blocks."

As Jim was finishing that story I hit my tee shot to the right into the trees. But there was not going to be a bad finish to a career round of golf. My ball hit a tree and kicked back into the golf course. Ken Venturi remarked that it was good that I "got away with it," and he said I had "made the right decision" to go with the driver instead of a three-wood. Who knows what he might have said had my ball stayed in the trees.

Before I hit, as I was going through my pre-shot routine, the graphic on the television listed Horton Smith in 1934, Gene Sarazen in 1935 and Fuzzy Zoeller in 1979 as the only three players who won playing in their first Masters. Surely a great way to jinx me, much like an appearance on the cover of Sports Illustrated magazine or a discussion of a no-hitter in the dug-out. I made a really hard swing at the ball and I got away with a slight block to the right. As I was watching the flight of the ball through a squint against the falling sun, I cracked a wry smile at just how hard I had swung. Still, nothing was fazing me, even as the ball was caroming off one of those stately Georgia pines that line the right side of number eighteen.

The pin was all the way in the back of the eighteenth green. I made a really good swing on my approach, but the ball came up short, leaving me with a long, difficult birdie putt. As Jim Nantz said, "that ball ends where you want it tomorrow for that traditional Sunday placement." I killed my first putt a good eight feet past the hole as Ken Venturi pleaded with the ball to "slow down." It would have changed everything had I missed the putt coming back. Jim Nance and Ken Venturi had some fun with it, but not as much as I did:

> JN: "Speaking of difficult two-putts . . . ."
>
> KV: "I know he made the long putt at sixteen, but all he's thinking right now is just get it close enough to the hole to two putt. Slow down! Slow down! You don't need to leave that one that long."
>
> JN: "H-m-m. He made the one seventeen. . . . ."
>
> JN: "Brian Henninger faces this putt for par."
>
> KV: "He's had six birdies today, two bogeys, and I know he wanted all of those putts, but I guarantee

you he wants this one most of all. He would like to stay in double figures. Just don't lose it to the left."

JN: "Oh ho! And that likely will put Henninger in the final two-some tomorrow."

KV: "And everybody's wondering how he can hit it so far."

JN: "Henninger, the Cinderella story this year."

As I shook hands with Davis, it hit me. Today was a special day. Not just a special day, a top ten or a top three-day. Certainly number one among my golf days. Since that day, I have come to appreciate even more what it meant to play the round with the consummate golf professional that is Davis Love, III. Davis is a great player. I was an upstart Masters rookie whom he could have chosen to ignore all day long. Instead, he held me up. All day long. For that, I am eternally grateful.

Jim Nantz was at it again as I headed for the special area set aside for turning in your scorecard. The carefully guarded sanctuary for the players to review and sign their cards has been around longer at Augusta than any other golf tournament because of Roberto DeVicenzo's scorecard disaster at the 1968 Masters. Mr. DeVicenzo had played one of the best final rounds in Masters history. He shot 31 on the front nine and finished with a 65. It was his 45th birthday. He should have played off against Champion Bob Goalby for the title. Instead, his playing partner, Tommy Aaron, had written a par 4 on the scorecard for the seventeenth hole. Mr. DeVicenzo had actually made a birdie 3. He failed to catch the error before he signed the incorrect scorecard. Under the Rules of Golf, the 4 was posted on seventeen, giving Mr. DeVicenzo a 66 and second place. "What a stupid I am," the Argentine gentleman was quoted as saying afterward. He was a British Open champion and a great player. He bounced back to win the Houston Open, three weeks after the debacle at Augusta.

CBS was replaying my reaction to the putt going in at sixteen and Jim Nantz described it as "the joyful exuberance of Brian Henninger, sharing the lead with Ben Crenshaw at the moment." I had made my way to the place all of us that play the Tour aspire to visit. The Butler Cabin. I heard Jim's voice on the monitor: "Back down to Butler Cabin. Bill McAtee:"

> BMc: "All-right Jim, thank you very much. With Brian Henninger, one of our co-leaders. Since that time, you have played the golf course in fourteen under par and they say Masters rookies are not supposed to be able to do that."
>
> BHH: "I know, I'll tell you what, Bill. When I started out on Thursday, I was the most nervous kid that you have ever seen on the first tee. I kept trying to shake it off. I was four over after five and I was fortunate, I hit it about a foot on six and I think that relieved a little tension. I didn't know what I was going to shoot but at least I had made a birdie and done something good."

BMc: "But you played yourself back into it. Let's take a look at your putt at sixteen. Talk us through it."

BHH: "Well, I practiced this putt in the practice rounds and it was probably the most difficult putt because the speed is so difficult. And, I played it up about three feet to the left. And I couldn't believe I made it. Because more than anything, I wanted it to get back up on top and stop. Because it will go by the hole and straight back down. I practiced it. I have studied this tournament and I watched the tournament a lot as a kid. I can hear the echoes of Norman and Nicklaus and Snead and Palmer down there around the corner. I remember so many golf shots. And the creativity and the imagination is there for me. I am seeing things well. I am seeing the speed and the line. My imagination is great right now."

BMc: "You were a tennis player. You didn't even start playing competitive golf until your junior or senior year in high school. You were a walk on at USC in southern California and now you have walked on to Augusta National and after three rounds, you are ten under par and are one of our co-leaders. You had missed your last two cuts coming in. Did you think that you would be in this position late Saturday?"

BHH: "Not at all. Actually, physically I have been striking the ball well this year. I think that having won at the Deposit Guaranty last year and finishing second at Atlanta, my expectations got carried away a little bit this year. I wanted to come out and I wanted to get to the next level. I wanted to be a guy that was reckoned with every weekend. That wasn't happening and my putting kind of got a little slow and its been real frustrating. And I haven't played very well the last few weeks. Even though I have made a lot of week-ends. Hopefully, you know, my putting is there right now. You never know, maybe the Golfing Gods will be here with me at Augusta."

BMc: "Brian Henninger, congratulations. Ten under par. We'll be looking forward to your round tomorrow."

BHH: "Thank you."

BMc: "All-right, let's send you back to eighteen."

JN: "And we'll find out here if Henninger will go into the night with a piece of the lead, or if Crenshaw will have the lead through three rounds. This for birdie."

KV: "No. That's about as bad as you can misread a green that Ben did there. He may have pushed it, but that's a fooler."

JN: "And a round without a blemish. Three birdies, fifteen pars, 69 Crenshaw."

KV: "You think they like him here?"

JN: "He is loved."

KV: "What an ovation he had. I'll tell you. Brian Henninger has handled himself so well. What is there not to like about him or root for him. He is just in awe of being here at the Masters."

Jim Nantz and Ken Venturi summed up the round Saturday evening with this:

JN: "So, at the 54 hole mark, the co-leaders are Brian Henninger and Ben Crenshaw. Eighteen players within five shots, twelve players within three of the lead. Henninger, Crenshaw, then Couples, Elkington, Mickelson, Hoch and Haas."

KV: "And then you've got some explosive players sitting right back here. Look at the round of Strange today, and Norman and Love with that length. And Houston, what a come back that was Jim."

JN: "Strange with the day's low round, 65. Mark McCumber, today, shot 69, three putting eighteen for bogey. Nick Faldo, doubled the sixteenth, otherwise, Faldo would be right on the edge of the lead. Tom Watson, 69."

KV: "Had too many bogies though. Ian Woosnam and he played, they were making birdies, but too many bogies. Azinger had it going but then lost it again. But its nice to see him back playing again, Jim."

JN: "Kenny Perry. Only inches away from an ace at twelve. Jack Nicklaus. You just take away that 78."

KV: "And Seve Ballesteros, trying to get back, Jim."

JN: "Tiger Woods. The 19 year-old freshman from Stanford, making the cut in his first Masters. There they are, Henninger, Crenshaw, Couples and others, right behind."

As I left the Butler Cabin, I was done. Drained. And it felt like it could get no better than that. I thought: "So why don't we all just say our good graces, do our interviews and go home?" Really. I had never achieved any more than I achieved that day. And, I had never before, nor since, experienced that much calmness and had that much fun playing tournament golf at any level. I never felt pressure that day. I was enjoying the walk. But I knew the pressure was coming. Ominously, I realized that with the pressure, the nerves would also return.

CHAPTER TWO

Who is That Little Guy? He Looks so Young!

*"That Brian Henninger hits it a mile!
And he's no bigger than my leg."*

Peter Jacobsen, October 15, 2001

I must pay homage to Peter Jacobsen before I discuss my family, friends and certain other facets of my life that make me who I am. Peter is my big brother on Tour, a role that he has played for many a young player that was wise enough to welcome Peter's help, insight and advice. I owe Peter Jacobsen a great deal, for which he will probably never be paid-in-full.

From a pure golf perspective, I owe Peter for inviting me to participate in so many of his Fred Meyer Challenge golf tournaments. That tournament, called "the finest Monday Pro-Am ever put together" by many golf insiders and pundits, put a lot of money in my bank account. It also allowed me to rub shoulders with many of the best players in the world.

Peter is an amazing guy, and he never forgets where he came from or how great it is to pull for the underdog. Peter, in his own way, intervened when the PGA Tour was getting a black eye for locking up with Casey Martin in the federal court lawsuit in Eugene, Oregon over whether the Americans With Disabilities Act applied to the Tour and would allow Casey, with his badly deformed leg, to use a golf cart to play on Tour. Various polls were taken of the players and substantially less than fifty percent sided with Casey. We all knew where Mr. Palmer, Mr. Nicklaus and Tim Finchem, the Commissioner stood on the issue. Casey's plight was an assault on golf's ability to make and enforce its own rules. Someone asked me recently why Peter or I did not take a stand here locally, or for that matter, why very few tour players that sided with Casey would speak up. There was an awful lot of peer pressure. The giant figures of Mr. Palmer and Mr. Nicklaus cast huge shadows. And you really didn't want to take a stand against the Tour when your livelihood depended on it. Just ask Jane Blaylock how much fun that can be, or read her terrific book The Guts to Win (with Dwayne Netland, Simon & Schuster 1977).

Peter did the next best thing. He invited Casey Martin to compete for the title in the field of the Fred Meyer Challenge, and to go head-to-head with the King and the Bear themselves. Even though U.S. Magistrate Judge Tom Coffin ultimately held for Casey and that decision stood up on appeal, the whole thing was terribly unfair. Judge Coffin was not a golfer, unlike several of the federal judges in the District of Oregon such as the Honorable Garr M. King, Senior Judge Owen M. Panner who regularly shoots his age or better, and Senior Judge Robert E. Jones, whose friends on the golf course, get to call him "Bobby Jones." The high-powered guy that argued the case for the Tour took offense at Judge Coffin's questioning of him during closing argument. All he wanted to do was put on his highly produced power point presentation and stick to the script. Too much technology. The Tour lawyers probably thought it was a disadvantage to have a non-golfer sitting in judgment.

The Tour does not have to worry about the decision as precedent because the court resolved the case on its own unique facts. And there will not be very many Casey Martins that come along knocking on the Tour's door. To me, it is most unfortunate because you have to wonder with Casey's God-given talent and the obstacles he has had to overcome, where he would be now if the Tour had instead chosen to embrace and support him. Would he have been more comfortable out there, the year that he finally obtained his PGA Tour card, and would he have had more success?

The most important thing Peter taught me was to appreciate everything I have as a professional golfer. He showed me how important it is to always go out of my way to treat other people well. Especially because you never know how or when that kindness will be repaid some day. Many times I have heard it said that I am a "great Pro-Am draw," meaning that the amateur or team of amateurs that is paired with me for a day on the golf course together will have a great day. I have worked very hard to earn that reputation and I am very proud of it. A great example that happened over the last two years makes Peter Jacobsen a prophet (he has been called "Saint Peter" and "Peter the Great" [only since the fall of the Berlin Wall] in the Portland area for the more than *ten million dollars* he has helped raise for charity). I have been struggling to get into events with only my current

Tour status as a "Past Champion." I have had some success writing letters to tournament directors and title sponsors seeking sponsor's exemptions into events for which I do not qualify. The fastest way to regain my Tour card is to get into an event, catch lightning in a bottle over the four days that count, and manage to win the golf tournament and the two-year exemption that goes with it. Gene Sauers pulled it off at the last staging of the Air Canada Tournament in British Columbia a few years ago. So can I. But, I digress. Here is the story that makes Peter Jacobsen a Prophet:

I met Seth Waugh, the Chairman of Deutsche Bank, playing in my favorite Pro-Am, The AT&T (formerly Bing Crosby's Clam Bake) at Pebble Beach, Cypress Point and Spyglass, near Carmel, California. We were paired together in the tournament a few years ago, and we became great friends. Deutsche Bank is now the title sponsor of a very big Tour stop held in Massachusetts over Labor Day week-end. In 2003, as part of my letter-writing campaign to tournament directors and sponsors, I wrote to Seth and asked for an exemption into the Deutsche Bank, which he graciously granted. Last year, I was too embarrassed to ask Seth again. I did not want to put a friend into the uncomfortable position of having to say: "Sorry, Brian, we have to give the spot to someone else this year." But Seth called me anyway, about a month before the tournament and said: "You know what, Brian, you are struggling and I want to help you out. Will you take one of our sponsor's exemptions this year?" What a great friend. And that Peter, what a great mentor.

The summer before my final year I met the woman of my dreams at a restaurant my father owned and operated in Eugene, Oregon. Cathy was studying interior architecture at the University of Oregon and her creative talents captured my interest immediately. She is also an artist which I found incredibly fascinating, primarily because that is where my talents end. In fact, my special awareness of fine art is about a 36 handicap. Our first date came the day I won the Pacific Coast Amateur at my home course, the Eugene Country Club, against a very strong field. It was probably Cathy's first footsteps on a golf course. We dated for three years and after winning the Queen Mary Open shooting 20-under par and breaking the tournament record by five strokes, I proposed to her in a quaint hotel in the Columbia Gorge. Basically, I finally had enough money to buy Cathy a ring. She is the backbone to my existence and without her I would have never accomplished nearly as much success. She is the mother of my three children and the soul mate of my dreams. It takes a special woman to take on the challenges of being a traveling companion to a professional golfer, and Cathy is that woman.

My life-long passion for the outdoors began on my Grandparents ranch as a little boy. A ten thousand acre ranch makes for a little boy's dream playground. The Hatfield Brothers ranch is a place I spent many a day shaping and molding my personality. Many life-lessons are learned hiking the creek bottoms in anticipation of catching a cutthroat trout, or setting a trap-line in anticipation of catching some kind of critter, or feeding a bummer lamb in the middle of the night pretending to be its mother, or helping in the hay fields with your little red wagon, which barely fit one bale of hay. I found my independence to be extremely entertaining and being "one with nature" was what I enjoyed the most.

Maybe these were the experiences that awoke my innate ability to rise to the occasion in competition. After growing up, I continued my outdoor adventures with my brother John. In the fall of each year, as the grind of the tour was wearing me out, I could always look forward with great anticipation to the fast approaching deer and elk seasons and sneaking around the Oregon Wilderness with John in search of big game trophies.

There were many a campfire that warmed our bodies after a long ride on horseback or the hard work of dragging our prey back to camp. Those were the "fireside chats" that I cherish the most.

My older sister Celeste has been a selfless supporter of my golf endeavors. Whenever the Tour landed at an event near Oregon, she was always there. At the Air Canada in Vancouver, at Pebble Beach and other California Tour stops, at Reno-Tahoe when I almost won the tournament, and of course, at every Fred Meyer Challenge. I could always count on Celeste to be supportive on and off the golf course. Celeste is as big a sports fan as am I, and our friendship often is surrounded by sports trivia. We are both huge Oregon Duck fans having grown up in Eugene, Oregon, and having a father that lives and breathes Duck athletics.

My father and mother have always been there for me and have been my two biggest fans. It was wonderful having them with me at Augusta National and having my father in attendance at my last Tour victory at Annandale Golf Club. Their unconditional love is always apparent, win or lose. I have had a lot of mentors and father figures over the years but I would never trade-in Wayne and Carolyn for anyone else.

Coach Randy Lein and Walking On at USC

I met Randy Lein in 1981. I had applied to USC and been accepted prior to ever hitting a golf ball in competition. Winning the Oregon State High School Golf Championship in 1981 gave me little credibility and there was very little interest from Division 1 schools. Especially one with the history of putting out tremendous golfers like USC. The spirits of Al Geiberger ("Mr. 59"), Craig Stadler, Scott Simpson, and other great players of less repute haunted vaunted Heritage Hall. I made contact with Ron Rhoads (the head coach) and made it clear that I was coming whether I made the team or not. I had a fascination with Southern California and felt it was important to challenge myself, leave the comfort and security of home, and to experience and explore education and life away from my family.

Randy replaced Ron Rhoades as the Head Coach in 1983. To this day he is the person most important to my success. He believed in me from the first day we shook hands and never has deviated from that belief. He opened the door to a kid that had tremendous up-side but very little ability. In today's era I would have never had the opportunity to make the USC golf team. Walk-ons are a thing of the past. My skills were limited, having only had one year of competitive experience, and the other guys playing on the team had refined and very educated golf games. To be completely honest, I don't believe I had ever had a golf lesson from a teaching professional. Randy was my guru and still is. I spent countless hours with him by my side. Randy always emphasized hard work, desire, dedication and confidence. Almost every weekend that I was not studying for important exams, I drove to little Westlake, California and played at North Ranch Country Club to hone my skills. Randy always made himself available. My last year at USC, having played out my eligibility but still wanting to achieve my educational endeavor, Randy invited me to live with him. I continued my studies and practiced to get ready for life and professional golf after USC. Randy even got me a job at Wilshire Country Club picking range balls so I could have practice privileges. While other graduating seniors were chasing love and libation, I was out there in the dark working on my swing under the lights of the range picker. I graduated and started the pursuit of my dreams.

Private Housing and My Other Families Out There

In my early years as a professional, 1990, 1991 and 1992, it would have been impossible for me to afford to go out on tour if I was not able to stay in private housing. A number of wonderful families opened their homes to me and several other Hogan Tour players. These relationships continue to this day. When I play in Jackson, Mississippi every fall, I stay with Andy and

Christy Wimberly who have opened their home to me for the last five years, ever since I won the 1999 Southern Farm Bureau Classic. Andy was the Chairman of the golf tournament. I can always count on the Wimberlys to bring a full entourage of friends and supporters to watch me play.

The "Almost Never Was" at New Haven, Connecticut

I was dead broke, and playing my first full year on the Ben Hogan Tour in 1991. I had Cathy come out to caddy with me. I decided I was going to train her to caddy to save some money. She left her job as an interior architect behind in Oregon and met me at the tour stop in New Haven, Connecticut, played over a terrific old links style golf course, the Yale University Golf Club. We went over the basics of caddying on the driving range and during the practice round.

We started out okay the first day by making par on number one. On the second hole, I pulled my drive off into the rough on the left-side of the fairway. The rough at Yale was very rough indeed. There were some boulders buried in the ground, here and there. My ball had come to rest about eight inches behind one of these boulders that had about a ten-inch high lip sticking up out of the ground blocking my path. This boulder was no loose impediment like the one Tiger had moved by members of the gallery a few years ago. It was firmly buried and it would have taken a back-hoe to get it out of the ground.

Because the rock was not sticking very far up above my ball, and because my short game was so pathetic, I had to find a club with enough loft to clear the rock, but enough carry to get me to the green. Cathy is so nervous, she is not even talking to me. She is just trying to figure out how to carry this big staff bag around. We are not having the typical caddy-player discourse. She is just allowing me to pull clubs out of there without any understanding that the rock is in my way and without reminding me I need to be sure and take enough loft. But how on earth could she have known to do that? Hitting over buried rocks was not part of our "caddying 101" session the day before.

So I took a full swing with an 8-iron and caught it flush so that it would have plenty to reach the green. The ball hits the lip of the rock squarely and ricochets at mach speed back in my direction, slamming directly into my left testicle. I instantly think the thing has exploded. I cannot breathe, and I can't talk. Cathy thinks I have broken my arm. I hobble a few feet over to the bushes and drop my pants to see if the thing really has exploded. It is all red and pulsating, and it is filling up with blood. In no time, it is as big as a baseball and growing. So I pull my pants up and hobble back out of the bushes. I still can't really talk.

"Did you break your arm?" Cathy implores. "Brian, did you break your leg? What did you do?"

Through clenched teeth, I manage to grimace out the words "I hit my balls."

"What?" She says, "I didn't hear what you said."

"I hit my balls!"

So we had an ambulance come out on the golf course and take me to Yale University Hospital. Fortunately, I did not need surgery. This was an episode, very early in my career, of what I like to call "what almost never was." But I survived New Haven, and the 1991 Hogan Tour, making an average of $1,088 for each of the ten cuts I made out of twenty-seven golf tournaments. Needless to say, I missed the cut at New Haven.

The Legend of the La Quinta Bag-Room Boy

One of the stories I really love to hear about my past is when someone with work experience on their resume that includes working at a fancy golf club tells me they have heard the "Legend of Brian Henninger." It is the story of a young golfer that made it out of the bag-room at La Quinta Country Club near Palm Springs, California. In 1990, after failing to get through the European Qualifying School, I went back to work for six months in the bag-room at La Quinta. Since I made it all the way to the big Tour, I have been told they still believe down at La Quinta that any bag-room boy can make it, and the sky is the limit.

Because of my work experiences at La Quinta, wherever my golf profession has taken me, I have always treated the shop and bag-room staff with the utmost respect. Indeed, I get as much enjoyment out of treating them well as I do treating the special people well. There were several times when we would bust our butts for guys that drove Ferraris or those big Mercedes Benz sedans (in the 1980s, it could have been Caddys or Lincolns) and receive nary a thin dime, even though we worked primarily for tips. After I made it out on Tour, as we worked our way through southern California on the West Coast Swing, I would run across a member or two from those by-gone days: "Hey Brian, remember me from La Quinta?" Under my breath, I would always say: "Yeah, I remember you, you schmuck, I worked hard for you for no tip." But I never say it out loud. I give a pleasant smile, or shake the guy's hand and move on. Peter Jacobsen has taught me well, and I like to think I am a good student.

Still, the way I get even is by going out of my way to be nice to the staff and to tip appropriately for a job well done. And I can tell you, there are not very many sloppy shoe shines or club cleanings when you reach my level. Also, it is very rewarding to give encouragement to the bag-room boys that I meet at least once or twice a year, struggling to make their way up tournament golf's ladder of success.

CHAPTER THREE

My Ticket to the Masters

"I love the idea that I'm in the Masters and that I have a two-year exemption. But my goal is still to go out and win a seventy-two-hole tournament."

Brian Henninger after winning the 1994 Deposit Guaranty Classic as recounted in A Good Walk Spoiled, John Feinstein, p. 410 (Little Brown, 1995)

The 1994 Deposit Guaranty Classic

My first PGA Tour victory sure did not feel like a real victory. I won the rain-soaked Deposit-Guaranty Classic at Annandale Golf Club in Jackson Mississippi. The tournament was shortened to 36 holes, and we were lucky to get that many in. I won by making a birdie on the first hole of a playoff with Mike Sullivan. It was the first time the tournament, formerly known as the Magnolia Classic, contested in Hattiesburg, had full PGA Tour Event status. That meant a two-year exemption to the winner and eighteen percent of the $700,000 purse or $126,000. And, as I learned shortly after I won, a victory at Annandale that year meant a ticket to the 1995 Masters Tournament.

During 1994, I was fortunate to meet John Feinstein, the great writer of sports books for young and old, golfer and non-golfer, rabid sports fan or someone just curious about sports. John is a master of his craft, and I was flattered and honored to be a part of his masterpiece about the 1994 golf season, A Good Walk Spoiled: Days and Nights on the PGA Tour (Little, Brown 1995). It was an enriching, highly educational experience to work with John as he followed my friends Paul Goydos, Jeff Cook and me around the 1993 PGA Tour Qualifying School and at times during the 1994 season. If you have not read John's book, you must. I hope he reads this little book, especially the parts about Bandon Dunes and the Fireside Chat, and he comes to visit us one October at Bandon. It would be marvelous if a writer of John's talent could be commissioned to write the book about that magical place.

At pages 409 and 410 of A Good Walk Spoiled, after telling us about Nick Price living his dream of handing his mother the claret jug after his thrilling victory at the 1994 Open Championship, John recounts the story of my first Tour win as follows:

> "On the other side of the ocean, real life went on. The PGA Tour always held an event opposite the British Open for those who didn't qualify for the tournament and those who didn't choose to go. Once, the tournament had been held in Chattanooga. Now Chattanooga was gone, replaced by the tournament that had in the past been held the same week as the Masters: the Deposit Guaranty Classic, which had been moved from Hattiesburg, Mississippi, to Jackson.
>
> The prize money--$700,0000—was the smallest on tour all year, but the event carried the same two-year exemption as any other for the winner and the

same ticket to the Masters, the World Series of Golf, and the Tournament of Champions.

The winner of all those extras, in addition to the $126,000 first prize, was Brian Henninger. His first PGA Tour victory didn't turn out exactly the way Henninger had envisioned it. He won the tournament on a soggy Sunday morning by winning a playoff from Mike Sullivan after tournament officials had determined that the golf course, drenched from three days of on-again, off-again downpours, was not going to be playable that day. Henninger and Sullivan had been tied for the lead after thirty-six holes, so they were brought back to the course to play off.

The only hole that was even close to playable was the 18th. Henninger and Sullivan were told they would keep playing the hole until someone won. As it was, eighteen was soggy and drenched. Henninger got it over with quickly, rolling in an 18-foot birdie putt. There was no gallery, no television, no one screaming for John Daly. But it was a win.

Henninger told the media that he was thrilled and proud to be the Deposit Guaranty champion, but he wouldn't feel as if he had really won on tour until he won a seventy-two-hole tournament. A number of players read those comments that week and were impressed. Billy Andrade made a point of telling Henninger when he saw him the next week that what he said had merit, but he should never feel as if he hadn't earned the victory. "You can only do what they give you the chance to do," he said.

When he finished with the media, Henninger called Cathy at home. His mother answered the phone since she and Brian's father were visiting. Thinking that Brian was about to go out and play his final round, she chattered on about how cute the baby was and how much fun they were having. Finally, Brian broke in.

'Mom, I won the golf tournament,' he said.

'You what? But how?'

He explained what happened. Everyone was thrilled . . . sort of. 'I love the idea that I'm in the Masters and that I have a two-year exemption,' he said. 'But my goal is still to go out and win a seventy-two-hole tournament.'

At least now he knew he would be able to play anywhere he wanted to go through 1996 in search of that goal."

To be completely honest, the winner's check was more important to me than the Masters invitation that rainy day at the Deposit Guaranty Classic. But, when I found out I got to go to Augusta, it was the ice cream on top of the cake.

The Annandale Golf Course and Jackson, Mississippi are truly special to me. I won again there in 1999 with my Dad following me at the tournament re-named "The Southern Farm Bureau Classic." That tournament was also shortened—to 54 holes, because it was contested over the weekend of Payne Stewart's memorial service. There was no playoff, but I was locked in a duel right down to the final hole with Chris DiMarco, a good friend from the Ben Hogan Tour. This time, first place money was $360,000 but there was no ticket to Augusta National.

More on all that, later. Now its time for some more about the key events leading up to that first win in 1994 and the twists and turns that got me to Augusta in 1995. There were several times that the train could have derailed entirely, with my golf game added to the trash heap of broken dreams.

Financing My Fledgling Career and my Three Wins on the Ben Hogan Tour

For several reasons, and because of many weird events, I almost never made it to the 1994 Deposit Guaranty Classic. The incident at New Haven ranks up there. And, also near the top of the list was my precarious financial condition when I turned pro in 1990 that did not improve much through my first full season on the Ben Hogan Tour in 1991. There are hundreds of stories about guys like me who try to raise money to finance their assault on the PGA Tour. Indeed, the late "Champagne" Tony Lema wrote about the phenomenon in 1964, more than thirty years before my first drive down Magnolia Lane, back when the pros played for $2,500,000 over the entire Tour season!:

> "There must have been a million ways of getting financial help. Players like Bo Wininger and Bob

McCallister draw salaries for doing public relations work for their backers. . . . I also heard of one rookie who must have figured he was quite a wheeler and dealer. Before setting out on the tour, he sold shares in himself. Unfortunately, he was a little too enthusiastic and sold 125 percent. He exhausted the nest egg soon enough, but every time he won $100 in prize money, he had to pay out $125. It was a lot cheaper not to win a dime so he dropped off the tour for a while to do some refinancing."

Golfer's Gold, Anthony David Lema (with Gwilym S. Brown) p. 158 (Little Brown 1964). Sadly, golf fans lost their opportunity to watch the development of an "All-American Big Three" when the super-talented Tony Lema and his wife Betty perished in a plane crash in 1966.

My story of high finance begins in the grill room of the Eugene Country Club in Eugene, Oregon in 1991, toward the end of the Hogan Tour season. It was shortly after the incident in New Haven, Connecticut, and I was out of money. Cathy and I were in Maine, with another great host family, and I got on the telephone to Eugene. I reached Steve Nosler, now the head golf coach of the University of Oregon Fighting Ducks, in the men's bar. After I told Steve my predicament, he passed the hat around Eugene Country Club and that helped us finish the 1991 season.

I desperately wanted to play the Hogan Tour full-time again in 1992, after not playing so well in 1991. That, year, I played in 27 events, had no top 10s, five top 25s and made only $10,878 in prize money. It was an improvement though, over the two Hogan events I played in during 1990 (winning $2,325) and the living we eked out that year from mini-tour pot game wins. I had just returned to Eugene from the first 1992 Hogan Tour event in Yuma, Arizona where I missed the cut. The next event, the South Texas Open in Corpus Christi, was two weeks away. I was dead broke. Broke as a church-mouse.

About two months before the 1992 Hogan Tour began, I applied some of the business planning education I received at the University of Southern California and put together a proposal with the help of an attorney and an accountant. Basically, I sold shares in me, and if I played well and made some money, my owners and I would split at the end of the two or three years. I spoke to several guys at the Eugene Country Club, visited doctors and lawyers that I knew of, and I knocked on a lot of doors. The Sunday before I was to leave to go back to the tour in Corpus Christi, Texas, I had a lot of promises but absolutely no money in the bank. I was sitting in the men's bar at the Eugene Country Club, not at all sure what I was going to do. In walked Cordy Jensen, a long time friend of my family and one of my supporters.

"Hey Cordy," I said, "I have all these commitments from doctors and lawyers, and other nice people here at the Club, but I have no money in the bank account we set up for this business endeavor. And, I'm the fifth alternate at Corpus Christi this weekend."

"No money," he said. "No problem." And Cordy reached into his pocket and handed me ten $100 bills.

I packed my car to the gills and drove south well before dawn on Monday morning. Cathy was going to join me on tour later, once she quit her job and closed up our apartment. I plotted a path on the Atlas through Nevada, Arizona, and then all the way to the bottom of Texas. By lunch time, I stopped at a little restaurant and casino, somewhere in Nevada. (I was not interested in gambling, only eating. I eat a lot for a guy that is five feet-eight, 140 pounds). About three hours down the road I have to stop for gas. When I look for my wallet, I can't find it, despite frantically searching for what seemed like at least 45 minutes. And, in light of my alternate status, if I happen to get into the golf tournament, I have to stick to my tight driving schedule. I call the restaurant, and thank God, they have the wallet and the cash. So I call Cathy and she says: "Proceed to Kingman, Arizona, to her Grandma Minnie's house. She is on the way." So I find Grandma Minnie and she gives me $200. I write her a check that she promises to hold until I can put some cash in the account.

I jump back in the car and drive all night. Early the next morning, somewhere in southern Arizona near Yuma, I get pulled over by a state trooper. He makes me feel like I am going to the cell block for sure, as I have no driver's license and no identification of any kind. I told him I played golf, and I had to make it to Corpus Christi in time for the start of the next tournament. I pleaded with him to let me go; I offered him golf balls, hats, a visor, anything in my car if he could see his way clear to allow me to continue my odyssey. He lets me go with a stern warning that the cops in Texas will likely just throw me in jail under these circumstances, and so I better slow down.

I drive straight through to Corpus Christi without incident and stay with another very nice host family. I tee it up on time, and proceed to win the golf tournament in a play-off with Bob Burns over one extra hole. I should have won in regulation, but could not capitalize on that opportunity. It would have been so easy to blow the whole thing. I had no money in my pockets, I have a one-shot lead playing the par-5 last hole with a green that is completely surrounded by water. I hit two perfect lay up shots. The pin is tucked back-left, so I try to keep it short of the hole. I one-hop my wedge over the back into the water and make bogey, causing the tie with Bob Burns and the playoff. No matter, I birdied the first extra hole, win the tournament and the $20,000 first place money.

Suddenly, I have a whole lot of guys, benefactors if you will, back in Eugene who remembered that they had purchased shares in my investment pool. Even though the only guy who gave me a nickel was Cordy Jensen, and his thousand dollars was sitting in a restaurant in Nevada.

The next thing you know, the investment bank account was full of real money. The very next day, in fact. I think I raised about $30,000. If I had not won at Corpus Christi, the $1,000 Cordy advanced me probably would have been the account's high watermark.

I won two more times on the Hogan Tour in 1992. In fact, I made three cuts in the first nine tournaments and won all three. Those three victories introduced me to the concept of the self-fulfilling prophecy. When you start to win, you start to believe you are the best. You continue to go down that road, and suddenly, you are the best at that time and in that place. And, you feel it every week and everybody around you feels it for you. You step on the tee and your feel like you "are the man." I know that is how Tiger Woods feels.

My Hogan Tour accomplishments were sufficient under PGA Tour rules at the time to earn me my very first Tour card for the 1993 season. That set up my emotional drive through the gates at the Hawaiian Open, where I met the late, great Payne Stewart for the first time.

Joining the Callaway Golf Team

The first time I ever met anyone from Callaway Golf was in 1992 at the Macon, Georgia Hogan Tour stop. One of my three wins on that tour that year. I met a Callaway equipment representative who was handing out the new Callaway metal head bore-through technology driver. I was signed with Ping at the time, and was carrying a Ping staff bag and wearing a Ping visor. But I was intrigued by the bore-through, and my contract with Ping allowed it, so I played that driver for the rest of the season. Callaway was still a fledgling golf club maker, and was not yet signing a lot of Tour players on to staff. The specialty at Callaway was still wood-shafted wedges and putters, made with Richard C. Helmstetter's custom pool–cue technology. Remember, "Big Jim", that "pool shootin's son-of-a-gun" in Jim Croce's "Don't Mess Around With Jim" had a custom pool cue. I bet it was one of Dick's.

So I was playing at Fort Smith, California, the last stop on the Hogan Tour that season. Tim Finchem, not yet Commissioner of the PGA Tour, who was working under Deane Beman, came out to hand those of us that had qualified our PGA Tour cards for 1993. That week, while hitting balls on the driving range, I turned around and saw Richard C. Helmstetter sitting in the stands in a straw hat. He looked important and he stood out. He came over and introduced himself. He looked very formal and interesting, with his neatly trimmed goatee and silver hair. He shook my hand and thanked me for using the Callaway driver.

Then, Mr. Helmstetter asked me if I would hit the club he was holding in his hand. A Callaway "Heaven-Wood." I said sure. It was a new and incredible experience. Now I was hitting a metal seven-wood that was surely the easiest-to-hit club I had ever tried in my life. Dick asked me if I would ever consider using the club in tour events and I said: "Absolutely."

At that point, either an ESPN crew or PGA Tour Productions video crew that was covering the granting of the Tour cards came up and wanted to do a little golf info-mercial with me on camera. So I grabbed Dick-son and the Heaven Wood and headed for the camera. I began to call him "Dick-son" after I learned of his prior life in Japan where he lived for many years, raised his children and became famous for making custom wooden pool cues. I believe that is one of the reasons Ely Callaway hired him—because he could make perfectly round, smooth, precision pool cues and Callaway Golf was becoming famous for perfectly round, smooth precision wooden shafts in putters and wedges.

"Mr. Helmstetter," I said, "how about I do this infor-mercial with the Heaven-wood?" I was really having fun with that club. My relationships with both Callaway Golf and Dick Helmstetter started right there and both have grown much stronger ever since. Had it not been for Callaway, professional golf would not have been the same wonderful experience for me that it has been for almost fifteen years. Within the next few weeks, I had to make what turned out to be that all-important life-enriching decision. Callaway sales were growing dramatically, and the company had begun to put together its pro staff at the same time I was getting ready to go out for my rookie season in 1993. I had to choose between Ping, a company that had been very good to me, and Callaway that was offering the opportunity to be part of something brand new and different. I chose Callaway in part, because I was intrigued by brand new and different. But mainly because of Dick Helmstetter and Ely Callaway. In the end, relationships mean the most to me. Like my relationship with my first agent, Bill Bentley, a class-mate of mine at USC who helped me with my original contract with Callaway.

I was very fortunate to get to know Mr. Callaway very well over the nine or ten years, before his passing. I met him well before the introduction of the Big Bertha driver that transformed the company and began the space race that is modern golf club (and ball) technology. He was the Godfather of club invention and everything he did was overlaid with the concept that the game of golf should be fun. When Callaway went into the golf ball business in the late 1990s, every box of balls had a piece of paper in it bearing the imaginary "Rule 35" of the Rules of Golf which reads simply: " Enjoy the Game." Those simple words embody the paramount spirit of Callaway Golf.

I have participated in the launch of every new golf club that Callaway has ever made. And I am very proud of that. Even the illegal "ERC II" driver has a purpose. It allows the aging player to still hit it out there a few extra yards. Like with most things, there is a down side to ERC II. Dick Helmstetter and I, witnessed my co-author, Brent Summers, hit the ball too high on the face of the ERC II off the first tee at the Bridges. I have never seen a ball fly like that. On impact there was a funny sound and the ball took off like a knuckle ball over the first 100 yards and then dove straight down into the canyon between the tee box and the fairway. I was howling with laughter as Dick looked at me and said, "we have had a problem with that." He told Brent to tee up another one with the ball barely an inch off the ground. The second time, the trampoline worked and I am sure the ERC II stayed in Brent's bag. Arnold Palmer unjustifiably took a lot of grief for supporting the golf club when it came out. The U.S.G.A. was "deeply concerned" about the integrity of the game. What a lot of people do not know is the technology of the ERC II, the thin "trampoline" face, is legal overseas and here in the United States in any wood *but* the driver. Watch the kid from Chicago that you will read about in Chapter Seven hit it *out* of the Callaway Test Center range with legal technology, and you won't worry a bit about the integrity of the game any more.

I first met Mr. Callaway at the company when they flew me to Carlsbad just before the start of the 1993 season. I am still amazed by his creative personality and strong convictions about what he expected from his employees and the golfers who represented his company. I met him in his office and he told me:

> "Brian, I don't want you to be like those race-car drivers with all those patches and signs all over their suits and their cars. I want you to represent my company, and I want you to be exclusive to Callaway Golf."

From that day on, whether I have a golf club logo on my staff bag, or something else, I am mindful of Ely Callaway's wishes and I am a Callaway guy through and through. I think I always will be, because of those two individuals, Mr. Callaway and Mr. Helmstetter.

My Rookie Year on the PGA Tour

The first time I ever experienced Payne Stewart in person was my first day on the job as a PGA Tour rookie in 1993. I vividly remember driving through the gates into the Hawaiian Open with tears in my eyes at the joy and relief finally making it. Cathy was sitting in the car next to me and telling me: "You deserve it, Brian, you have worked very hard to get here."

So I parked the car and walked gingerly into the locker room to put my street shoes in my locker. I found my way to the driving range, which was really quite small. It could only fit about twenty players at a time, so

I stood there, fidgeting, waiting my turn. Again, I am walking on eggshells. I am young, I am emotional, I am nervous, I am scared, and I am really wondering if am good enough to be out here. I have watched all these great players on television. And here I am, waiting to hit balls with them.

I squeeze in between two guys with my head down. There is one right in front of me and one right behind, but I am too scared to look up and see who they are. I have my chin buried as I start my little practice routine. But I am able to notice that the person in front of me has this unbelievably fluid, beautiful golf swing. He has gotten up to his driver, and he is just lacing these perfect drives right down this narrow little corridor of a driving range. Every shot seems to be hitting this one big tree down at the end of the range.

I'm thinking, "God, is this guy ever good!" He turns around and it's Payne. I introduced myself, and he said: "Good to meet you, Brian, welcome to the PGA Tour." He was not wearing knickers, or one of those British pub caps he was so famous for. He was in khakis and a baseball cap, and I didn't even recognize him at first. Payne Stewart has been missed, and will continue to be missed for many, many years to come. His sheer talent was as incredible as the tempo of his golf swing. He added some color with his personality and outfits, and he had tremendous respect for the traditions of golf. And I was fortunate that he was a part of my first day as a PGA Tour player.

I have always had the feeling that I will do well at certain venues. The Western Open, staged at Cog-Hill near Chicago is one of those places. I have had some incredible rounds and some great results at the place that used be known as an "almost-major" because of the quality of the golf course and the tournament's fine traditions.

One of the great experiences I had in Chicago was during my rookie season in 1993. I was paired with Fred Couples and we were playing well, so we were in one of the last groups. It was one of my first big tournaments and my first big crowd. Because it was my rookie season, I am not getting to know many of the guys very well. I was kind of nervous, so I went over and shook Fred's hand and introduced myself. We were standing on the first tee at Cog-Hill and its ten people deep, clear around the tee box and clear around the green. Fred, being one of the more popular players, was used to all this. I was very nervous. But Fred was being extremely respectful of my rookieness and unease. He was being all of it at once, gracious, hospitable, friendly and kind. He recognized that I was a little bit out of my element, an element he was totally used to as they crawled all over and around him and the ropes every week he played. Anyway, I shot 68 that day and finished in fourth place. It was a huge payday for me and a great confidence-builder. For that I thank Fred, and his genuine support.

I lit up Cog-Hill in 1999, shooting 63 on Saturday to hold a share of the third round lead. I was very fortunate on Sunday to make it into the last group because I missed being paired with Tiger Woods, who was in the group in front of me. I am not saying that being paired with Tiger is a bad thing. I have had that experience and enjoyed it immensely. But at that time, everyone wanted to follow Tiger and pull for him. In a lot of ways, it's good energy for Tiger, and bad energy for his playing companion. There were very few people following my group that Sunday. But I sure do not blame them. When Tiger is playing and I am not, I am one to turn on the television because I love to watch him play. And of course I want to see if he can win another golf tournament.

Neither Tiger nor I won the golf tournament that day. I had a tough, disappointing round in the sweltering heat and humidity and finished tied for sixth. But the day before, on Saturday, when the order of play by Tiger and I was reversed and I shot 63, I had the experience of a lifetime. That day, Tiger was playing in the group behind me. Again, fortunately, Tiger had attracted most of the on-lookers. But there were still people camped around each of the greens. Tiger was watching and heard the cheers as I made birdie after birdie after birdie. He sought me out after the round was over and praised me for the incredible round that he had watched from the group behind. That makes you feel pretty good, coming from the greatest player on the planet. And, it will be something that Carlin, Hunter and Mia can tell their grandchildren. I was on a great high in 1999, still hands-down the best year of my pro career with a win, a third place, and two more top-tens to boot.

But once more, I must emphasize its all a building process. My success at Cog-Hill with Fred Couples does not happen without my three Hogan Tour wins. Success at the Bell South does not happen without Cog-Hill. I don't win at the Deposit Guaranty Classic without the charge at the Bell South. And, of course, the 1995 Masters success does not happen without the Deposit Guaranty Classic Victory. To borrow a phrase from Kurt Vonnegut: "And so it goes."

The 1994 Bell South Invitational ("Goliath Beat David—Barely") and Letting Superman Fly

John Feinstein named Chapter Fourteen of A Good Walk Spoiled "Goliath Beats David . . . Barely." Over pages 301 to 317, John chronicled the magic I experienced at the 1994 Bell South Invitational at Atlanta Country Club as I chased John Daly down the stretch. I said at the beginning of this book that my play at the final hole that day, and Ken Venturi's call of the action for CBS, made Sunday May 8, 1994 rank as the second most recognized golf event for which I am known by golf fans. The Bell South experience makes a pretty darn good runner-up, and I experienced a lot of the same feelings at Atlanta that I had on Saturday, April 8, 1995 at Augusta National. I finished second at Sugarloaf near Atlanta, Georgia in 1997. I seem to have a propensity to make fireworks go off in Georgia.

I was paired with John Daly. He was leading the tournament and was two strokes ahead of me as we stood on the tee of the par-5 eighteenth hole. John hit the longest drive in competition that I had ever seen in person at the time. There was a 115 year-old oak tree sitting in the way, out there about 270 yards. So for John to fly the ball over that tree, he had to hit it 300 yards in the air.

Not with today's technology, mind you, with spring of 1994 technology. The rest of us had to shape our tee shots around the tree and between the fairway bunkers if we wanted to have a chance of reaching the green in two shots.

I teed-off first and hit a perfect drive, leaving myself about 210 yards to the flagstick. John then creamed that huge drive. The gallery roared. People shrieked and hollered "you da man, John." Somewhere nearby, dogs howled and some people probably fainted. The ball flew right over the tree and he turned back toward me and gave me a grin that meant he had just hit his "Sunday Best." John's ball was at least 40, maybe 50 yards past my ball. He had only an 8-iron left to the green for his second shot.

I had 200 yards to carry the bunker, which was just over the lake, and about 212 yards to the hole. I chose a 4-iron and I had to fit the ball into a little tiny space on the back-left portion of the green. I hit the shot that I know Ken Venturi will always remember, because I watched the replay of the telecast in the locker room afterwards. Ken said something like: "Brian Henninger really needs to make a good check. He needs to hit the ball in the middle of the green and not worry about going for this pin."

At the time, money was indeed very important to me. But, winning was everything and this was a great opportunity. It was the competitive juices that flow in guys at my level that got me there in the first place--the difference between me and thousands of scratch or better golfers around the country. I was just going to try to hoist a 4-iron to that little spot. I would hit it as good as I could, and if the ball did not end up there, I would do my best to get it up and down and go on from there. The beauty of it was I was not thinking "result" as I swung. I did, however, manage to manufacture the best shot of my life in that situation and the ball landed softly on the green and ended up about eight feet past the hole.

John hit his second shot into the bunker on the right side of the green, so I had to wait for him to play first and he blasted the ball to about five feet. It was my turn. I had to putt first and I made it, shaking like a leaf. Every one who saw me hit the putt said later that I looked very calm. Little do they know watching through that mask of a television screen that most of us are very nervous in a situation like that.

To this day, though, I remain unable to explain why I was very, very nervous over that eight foot putt on the seventy-second-hole at The Bell South while I was calm and on cruise-control on Saturday at the 1995 Masters, with no nerves what-so-ever.

There have been extensive efforts to study nerves, brain-lock and other afflictions that imperil professional athletes when they are in contention for a large prize. Scott McCarron and I have a little saying for this, when either of us are contending for a title. We might call each other, leave a voice mail or a text message and say: "Let Superman Fly."

I did this study years ago, with Dr. Richard Coop and some Wake Forest students. They were studying brain waves. They put some headphones on me while they tried to measure the relationship between brain waves and sound. Thought and sound. They asked me to think about a lot of things, good and bad, such as my relationships, my hobbies, Cathy and my kids. Clearly, different thoughts create different sounds. Then, the students showed me this lap top computer with a little animated Superman stretched out flat in the flying position at the bottom of the screen. They said: "We want you to make Superman fly."

At the time, I was as confident in myself and my abilities as Tiger Woods was when he held all four major championship trophies at the same time. (Sadly, it is not limited to a confidence contest). I believed I could do anything, so I asked the students, before I started in, "Have you ever seen Superman fly on this thing?" The answer was "yes, we have." So I put on the headphones and shut my eyes. I thought I knew the answer. I had read the books and seen the movies about Superman. I would just visualize Superman flying through the buildings over New York City. For about two or three minutes I tried to see Superman flying in my mind, but I could not get the little animated guy up off of his belly.

I learned from the previous experiment that if I had no thought at all, there would be no sound. So I tried to implement no thoughts. I tried to find the dead space in transition from thought to thought and stay there. Every time there was a flash of thought, I tried not to think for a second. Every time I did that, Superman started to fly. So when I left that little experiment, I considered the no-thought state the alpha state. The supernatural or the peaceful mind, with no dialogue in there. Michael Jordan was there numerous times in his career. Jack Nicklaus had to have been there on the back-nine on Sunday at the 1986 Masters, which I consider to be the greatest achievement in golf, and perhaps in all sports. I think those are the supernatural states that all of us need to find to accomplish great things.

Of course, the cliché is "the Zone." And those students were studying "the Zone" with me that day. Scott McCarron and I consider that no-thought state where Superman flies to be the zone. Ever since I shared my experience with Scott, we have said: "Let Superman Fly tomorrow" when wishing each other good luck on the golf course. What we mean is don't get in your own way tomorrow. Enjoy the process uncluttered, and try not to think too much about result and all those things that can deter you from playing well.

So there I was, over the eight-footer for eagle on the final green at the Bell South. And Superman was *not* flying. The nerves were flying. What saved me though, was the confidence I had developed that week by putting very well around Atlanta Country Club. Even though I was very nervous, just laying my Zebra putter (the flavor of the month) down behind the ball gave me great confidence that I would make the putt. Also, thinking about result is not as deadly on the seventy-second-hole of the golf tournament. Especially when you are doing everything you can to come from two strokes-back. There are a limited number of outcomes and the tournament will be over soon. Prior to that time, when there are a lot of guys still out there with a lot of golf to be played, thinking too much about what you are doing and what the result is that you want or need can be very costly. It is impossible to control the outcome, so why try. On the last hole at the Bell South, I felt pretty much in control because of that 4-iron I had hit so pure and because I had putted well all week. Also, helping me out a great deal, was the fact that the putt was down-hill. It was also pretty straight. I have always said that if I have a putt to win a golf tournament, I want it to be down-hill. You do not have to apply any energy to the ball. You just have to keep the putter-face square somehow and just touch the ball to get it rolling. It will make it to the hole on its own. This one went right into the center of the cup.

Unfortunately, Big John made his five-footer for the win and there was no playoff. I love Ken Venturi to death, but I had some fun at his expense back in the locker room watching the replay: "Hey Ken, I am *not* going for the *middle* of the green. You don't win golf tournaments going for the *middle* of the green." Don't get me wrong; at the Masters in 1995, I would have given anything to have Mr. Venturi coach me through an ear piece around Augusta during Sunday's round. I believe it would have made a huge difference. And today, I factor in what the great commentators would say about a particularly delicate shot or difficult situation. It's all part of the evolution.

The BellSouth was a tremendous experience for me. I was paired with John Daly for the last two days. He and I basically led the golf tournament from wire-to-wire. And, I was able to carry all that good juice with me to other events, including the 1995 Masters. That is how I have lived my life on Tour--from golf tournament to golf tournament, and never too high, never too low.

John's five-footer was a pretty easy putt. But as he was picking up his coin and getting ready to putt, I honestly thought he would miss. He had not hit a very good bunker shot, and I just managed to turn up the pressure when my eight-footer disappeared into the bottom of the cup. But John showed the golf world once more just how great he was as he calmly rapped the ball into the middle of the hole. My reaction was much like I felt at the end of the third round at Augusta in 1995. I felt awesome. Even though I didn't win, it felt as though I had just won the golf tournament. Maybe that's why I have had some of the unique experiences I have had. I never let myself get too far down, because I know there has to be some more good stuff right around the corner.

That victory was very, very big for John. Also, I was very happy for him. He was another great player to be paired with under those circumstances. He hit some of the longest drives I have ever seen. I didn't even know a person could hit a golf ball as far as he did at that tournament. There was one hole at Sugarloaf that stands out even today. I think it was number nine, a sharp up-hill dogleg left, with 265 yards to the corner and another 180 yards straight up-hill to the green from there. John hit first, and I saw where I thought he was aiming-up over the hill and some trees, across the corner at the green. At first, I thought he was going to play a cut shot. But he smashes the ball way left and I think he is in the parking lot. A pang of happiness settles over me, as I am thinking Big John is just going to give me the golf tournament today, especially if he keeps trying to hit those crazy shots. And, I am feeling very good about my game. John starts walking up the fairway with me, and I want to say to him: "Hey John, you should be walking over there, toward the parking lot." I look over, where I think his ball should be, but it is not there. Instead, it is seventy yards short of the green, right in front in the fairway. With the dogleg routing, this hole plays about 445 yards, straight up-hill. As the crow flies, over John's ball flight, the distance to the hole is about 380 yards and still uphill. It was an incredible, drive.

John hit a couple of famous bombs when he participated in the Fred Meyer Challenge at the Oregon Golf Club in the mid-1990s. One year on the first tee, John teed it up well before Bill Schonely, the tournament announcer, and long-time voice of the Portland Trail Blazers was ready to call his name. John blasted a 330 yard carry up-hill, over the heads of the foursome marching up the fairway in front of him at the 270 yard mark. John also hit one off the top of a soda can over the top of the massive crowd assembled in a bowl-shaped amphitheater around the eighteenth green at the Oregon Golf Club during Peter Jacobsen's famous pre-tournament clinic and impression show. That was a colossal drive that had to get up in the air very quickly, or some spectator's surviving family members would have likely owned Big John's then net worth, the golf course property and the Fred Meyer Challenge, or certainly a large piece of their respective insurance carrier's cash positions.

John was great for golf when he crashed onto the international scene after winning the PGA at Crooked

Stick, his first major. I have always enjoyed watching him play, and it was an absolute privilege and a huge thrill to spend May 7 and 8, 1994 slugging it out with him at Atlanta Country Club.

CHAPTER FOUR

Arriving at Augusta National in Wide-Eyed Amazement

"One of the reason the Masters Tournament has become so special is the attention that is paid to every detail."

And then Jack Said to Arnie…
Don Wade (Contemporary Books 1991)

The Grounds

The turf at Augusta National was just so incredibly perfect for guys that like to practice. And, I like to practice very much. Now, my body has never held up to the type of practice sessions that Vijay Singh puts in. As a consequence, no one will ever tell stories about me hitting balls until my hands bleed. But I do take away a huge amount of satisfaction from a good practice session. I remember each day that I went out to practice at Augusta, I enjoyed it more than ever before because the turf was so good. Never better. The only golf course I have played that has turf conditions even close to Augusta is the Coeur d'Alene Resort on Lake Coeur d'Alene in Idaho. That is due to the fact that the greens-keeper is Jon Anderson, the guy with which Peter Jacobsen entrusted his dream design, the Oregon Golf Club.

Each day I went out to the range at Augusta, I found a different feel. It was never exactly the same and I was never working on any specific thing. I played competitive golf for years and years just going to the driving range and trying to find a feel. If I find a feel, I am going to go with it for the rest of the day. You can call it a swing key, or a swing component. But it's a feel. And that is how I prepared myself to play at Augusta in 1995 on that gorgeous turf, and at every other golf tournament before that.

Our Rental House

Instead of staying at the Best Western, I came to discover that what you do when you are playing in the Masters is you rent someone's home in Augusta, Georgia for the week. It is a lot more expensive, and that kind of made me nervous as well. I thought it was kind of peculiar that people would take their kids and go take a vacation while somebody stayed at their house. In fact, during the first 24 hours, it was very uncomfortable for me because the people don't take their things out of the houses. But I rented a home, complete with the baby-to-teenager photographs, and it worked out very well.

My Family, Friends and Only Six Tickets

Fifteen years ago, the prize money on the PGA Tour and the Ben Hogan Tour (now the Nationwide Tour) was no-where near what it is today. The only way I could afford to play on the satellite tours in 1990, where I did fairly well winning my share of the entry-fee split pot games, and the Hogan Tour after I performed well enough at the 1990 Q-School to get a Hogan Tour card, was to stay in private housing each week. The first year going around the Hogan Tour, I stayed with a lot of very nice families, but two stood out. The first event of the season was in Yuma, Arizona, where I stayed the Pasquinelli family. Then, as we made our way around the country and headed home, Texarkana was a tour stop and I stayed there with the David Whitt family. Both families became sponsors of mine. Gary and Barbara Pasquinelli are the Godparents of my daughter Carlin. Carlin's name came from David Whitt's daughter. All in all, these people were incredibly supportive and helped me a great deal in being successful.

At the Masters, you get six tickets. And, you are not qualified or capable of asking for any more. I had to sit down and really think about who was special to me. I think that is a very difficult task each and every year for the players to have to determine who gets to go enjoy the week with them. So I decided that these people, Gary and Barbara Pasquinelli and David and Ruth Ellen Whitt were very significant people in my life at that time and they deserved to see me play at Augusta in 1995. Of course, the remaining two tickets went to my parents, Wayne and Carolyn Henninger. Cathy's mom was also there, and she would exchange badges with Cathy as they took turns baby-sitting Carlin back at the rental house.

If I had been able to scare up two more tickets, no doubt they would have gone to my dear friend Nelson Clyde, III, the publisher of the Tyler, Texas Morning Telegraph. I met Nelson playing in a Pro-Am in Tyler. Nelson drew me in the blind draw for partners. I was the last pick in the draw, and Nelson had the last choice. Lucky for me. Nelson is the perfect father, or the perfect grandfather, or the perfect mentor. He is just one of those people that I want to embrace and hug and enjoy at dinner and on family outings. I spent a lot of time over the years with Nelson and his family. Another reason I really need to make it back to the Masters is so that I can give Nelson tickets. There is a whole lot to all of this that goes on beyond the ropes. And I am only touching on a few of the people here that have made my journey "following the sun," to borrow a phrase from yet another great golf book, so enjoyable. There have been many, many others.

Nelson always follows my career so closely, and given his newspaper background, he is quick to point it out when a publication makes a mistake about me. Here is an example of a letter to the editor of Golf World Magazine (May 30, 1997) Nelson wrote to correct the record:

Henninger's Eagle

> "My favorite rising star, Brian Henninger, has to love being in Georgia on the 18th with a downhill putt on Sunday afternoon in May. His Birdie to gain a second-place tie in the BellSouth Classic at the TPC at Sugarloaf was reminiscent of his eagle at Atlanta CC in 1994.
>
> However, the earlier eagle did not lift Henninger into a playoff, as CBS' Ken Venturi said in this year's reconstruction.
>
> After Henninger hit his famous 4-iron 212 yards over water to the 18th and made the eagle putt, he and

Nolan Henke were momentarily tied with John Daly. Daly won by making birdie from a greenside bunker."

My Practice Round With Larry Mize

Larry Mize was another veteran player and former Masters champion that was extremely kind to me during my first Masters experience. We played a practice round together and Larry was extremely forthcoming with valuable information about the wind, the driving lines and the greens. I also asked him to show me that famous spot from which he chipped in during the playoff in 1987 when he won the green jacket from Greg Norman and Seve Ballesteros.

My Practice Round With Dick Helmstetter

Dick Helmstetter was at the 1995 Masters. He had played the golf course before that, and he walked the entire day with me during one of my practice rounds. He told me to beware of this and beware of that. At the time, I had only known Dick since the fall of 1992, when I met him at the last of the Hogan Tour events that year. We were receiving our PGA Tour cards, and Dick was in the audience. He also introduced me to a new Callaway product there, the "Heaven-Wood," and he was a principal reason that I ended up signing with Callaway as I started my rookie season in 1993.

I am grateful to Dick for taking that much of an interest in my success to spend an entire day with me helping me to prepare at Augusta. It has been a unique and incredibly interesting experience every time I spend time with Dick-son. He has always been pretty proud of me, not only as a golfer, but as a person. And I have always looked up to Dick as a father-figure, a mentor and an advisor. One thing I am eternally grateful to Dick for is teaching me the difference between good red wine and bad red wine. And, how to find good red wine at a reasonable price. I am sure Dick ranks right up there with the world's best wine guys (I know there is a fancy word for it, but I couldn't find it before the press deadline). "Good wine guy" works for me.

Nervous on the Tee at the Par 3 Tournament

I have said many times that I was far more nervous anticipating an 80 yard wedge shot during the Par- 3 Tournament than at any time on the golf course during the tournament proper. Put a 5-iron in my hand and let me swing away, and it's certainly no big deal. But a three-quarter swing that is all carry over water in front of Sam Snead, Gene Sarazan and Byron Nelson? That's nerve-wracking and very difficult.

The Arnold Palmer Dedication

The amazing thing for me about the Arnold Palmer dedication that took place at Augusta National on April 4, 1995 was that I missed the ceremony. It was a Tuesday, and I was still wandering around the grounds in a daze, taking in all of the incredible sights and sounds of Augusta National. I first realized what I missed while watching the tapes of the 1995 telecast, especially the Sunday telecast, when Walter Cronkite did a tribute to the tradition of Masters, the fortieth telecast by CBS and the thirtieth anniversary of Mr. Palmer's first green jacket.

Jack Nicklaus Wins the 1986 Masters

In the press room Saturday evening after my interview with Bill McAtee in the Butler Cabin, I said my long putt at sixteen reminded me of the putt Jack Nicklaus made there in 1975 to launch him to victory over Tom Watson and Johnny Miller. I also said that Jack's victory at the Masters in 1986 was among the greatest, if not *the* greatest individual accomplishments in sports. I had said to Bill McAtee that my imagination was great and that I was seeing the line on my putts and the pathways to my chip shots very well on that special Saturday. Looking back at all of it, I believe that watching the Masters as a kid growing up, and rooting for Jack Nicklaus in particular, gave me something to draw on while I was out there playing in my first Masters in 1995.

In 1986, the Masters was enjoying its fiftieth anniversary. Jack Nicklaus was 46 years old when he beat Greg Norman and Tom Kite by one stroke to win his sixth green jacket. The spectacle that was the golf tournament that year is superbly chronicled in one of my favorite golf books, Stephen Goodwin's The Greatest Masters: The 1986 Masters & Golf's Elite (Harper & Row 1988). Over pages 125 to 127, Mr. Goodwin writes:

> "It had been a momentous day. Thousands of fans began to make their way slowly toward the exits, their voices still bubbling with excitement as they tried to describe the spectacular shots they'd seen, and the

emotions they'd felt as the plot unfolded. They all knew they'd just seen a thriller, a tournament that would be remembered and discussed for years to come. There were rebel yells and more high fives and happy outbursts everywhere, as fans congratulated themselves on having the good fortune to be present at Augusta National when the Golden Bear played what even he called the finest golf of his career. His 30 on the back nine had tied the course record, and his scorecard was something to behold:"

"444 443 453 – 35"
"334 443 234 – 30 – 65"

"To translate those numbers into words, he had played the last ten holes birdie, birdie, birdie, bogey, birdie, par, eagle, birdie, birdie, par. In the seventeen major championships he had previously won as a professional, he had never traveled at such a scorching pace over the closing holes."

"[In the press room] Nicklaus . . . went on to say that while he'd been struggling with his game, he had promised himself not to retire from golf on a low note. Anticipating the next question, he added, "I'm not retiring now guys, I'm not that smart.'"

"The interview continued for almost an hour. The writers scribbled away on their notepads, trying to figure out how they could possibly file a story that would do justice to the day's events. There was too much to tell—too many shots when the outcome of the tournament hung in the balance, too many stunning reversals of fortune. And somehow or other you had to reckon with the fact that Jack Nicklaus had now won twenty major championships, a figure that conjured up the dimensions of his epic career. The young Jack Nicklaus, growing up, had known only one golf statistic—that Bobby Jones had won thirteen majors. For several generations to come, young golfers will learn that jack Nicklaus won twenty major championships—unless, of course, he happens to win another."

I always remember that Greg Norman finished second to Jack Nicklaus's emotional charge in 1986. The very next year, Greg lost to Larry Mize's famous chip-in at number eleven, the second play-off hole. And, in 1995, nine years after the Bear's sixth victory at Augusta, Greg Norman finished third after making a great run following an opening round 73 with three 68s in a row from Friday to Sunday. This time, he finished third to Ben Crenshaw's emotion-packed perseverance. And, the very next year, on the tenth anniversary of the "Greatest Masters," the greatest driver of the ball ever, relinquished a six-stroke lead and the green jacket to Nick Faldo. I wish I could write as well as Stephen Goodwin, for I love his description of the "Great White Shark" at page 28 of The Greatest Masters:

"Greg Norman, a.k.a. the Great White Shark, the Australian with the shoulders of a stevedore and the waist of a dancer, was belting out the prodigious drives for which he was famous. He was also famous for his platinum hair, his cheerful irreverence, and his attacking style of play. Every time he sent a ball soaring into the distant nets—a small awestruck voice inside your head exclaimed, 'But that is huge! That is huge!' Norman himself seemed to savor his power as much as the fans, who kept urging him to drive one into Washington Road. One of the reasons for his enormous popularity, surely, was the unabashed gusto he brought to the game."

As I played the 1995 Masters, it is fair to say that I tried to drive the ball like Greg Norman and play with the imagination of the great Jack Nicklaus. The example set by those two consummate professionals over the years was the closest thing I had to a coach out there. My success was, for the most part, due to three factors: First, I did manage to drive the ball superbly. Second, with the exception of the weather on Thursday, the fact that Augusta National firmed up quickly and played hard and fast under ideal conditions enabled an inexperienced player like me to make a lot of birdies. Third, I was able to bring great imagination and vision to bear as I played the golf course. I firmly believe that following the Bear at Augusta on television all those years as a kid contributed a great deal to my ability to see things so clearly.

I had an experience of a lifetime near the end of Mr. Nicklaus' playing career on the regular Tour. I was paired with him for two days at New Orleans in 2001. Cathy was there, and we spent some quality time with Jack and Barbara. It was a dream come true. After watching him compete on television when I was a kid, and drawing on those telecasts at the 1995 Masters, it was like winning the lottery to be playing with the greatest player of all time in my chosen profession before he retired. And it was purely a stroke of good fortune to have the pairings computer spit my name out next to his for the Thursday and Friday rounds. I have played in one of Jack's Pro-Ams in Florida, where Glen Day and I got after each other on one of Jack's grass tennis courts. I have been around him at Tour events and of course, at the Fred Meyer Challenge. But nothing could compare to the experience of playing 36 holes in competition with Mr. Nicklaus at New Orleans. Thank you, Jack, for those two days.

Once again I have to chalk up a great deal of my success on Saturday to being paired with Davis Love. I was very happy for Davis when I learned that he was able to finish second to Ben Crenshaw. Writing this book, I had to look up who I had been paired with on Thursday, and it was Mike Springer. With the inclement weather conditions and my early round struggles, I could have been playing with the great Jack Nicklaus on Thursday and I still would have had to look it up. The sound of the rain hitting the umbrellas tends to pretty much block-out the sounds of everything and everyone else around you except the words you exchange with your caddie. On Friday, I do remember shooting my 68 paired with Nick Faldo. Wc had an awfully good shot-making day, and it was wonderful to be paired with such a master of the game. I am sure I owe a piece of that 68 to Mr. Faldo.

The calm tone in Davis Love's voice and the casual approach that he took to the day helped me feel like "hey, we're just a couple of buddies out here playing a nice casual round of golf." Never mind being at the greatest place to play on the planet, among the world's greatest golf fans. I think Davis's demeanor had a lot to do with my being so relaxed on Saturday. He made me feel like I belonged out there at Augusta and that I was good enough to be right there, in the hunt with him and the other star players at the top of the leader board.

I shook hands with Davis and I walked off the 18th green to the greeting of a CBS runner who was telling me they wanted me to go to the Butler Cabin and see Bill McAtee. I think it is every professional golfer's goal to see the inside of that place and be interviewed there. Of course, you really want to be the one there on Sundays, being helped into the green jacket by the previous champion. I have allowed myself to wonder, on an occasion or two, whether the Augusta National Tournament Committee ordered a diminutive version of the green jacket after my fireworks on Saturday. You know, just in case . . . .

Today, looking back, my trip to the Butler Cabin is hard to remember. Some of it comes back to me when I watch the interview on television. It seems it was all a great big blur. I was caught in a whirlwind. I do remember thinking as I shook hands with Bill McAtee, that the world is going to get to know me, whether they want to or not. Watching the telecast today, it also strikes me how much younger and thinner everybody looks. I have always been told I look a lot younger than I really am. I was 32 at the 1995 Masters, but people tell me I looked 21. And, I was skinny. I weighed no more than a hundred and forty pounds. I have no idea where Bobby Clampett came up with the extra fifteen pounds when he made the call at seventeen on Saturday and said I was five feet-eight, a hundred and fifty-five pounds.

CHAPTER FIVE

No Sleep, Sleeping on the Lead

"Davis Love, Faldo, Norman and Elkington. Those guys all had coaches. Swing coaches, head shrinkers—I didn't have a coach—I went to the driving range each day and tried to find a new feel."

Brian Henninger, March 21, 2005

I have been asked several times if I slept much on the lead that Saturday night in the rental house in Augusta. The answer has always been a resounding "No! Not at all." I tried several times to find sleep, but it would not come, so I was up making coffee and pacing around the kitchen well before sunrise. The big problem that never really struck me until mid-morning, was that my tee time was not until 2:00 o'clock that afternoon. Now, I really did not know what to do with myself. I thought about running over to the driving range at a nearby municipal golf course and running over the golf tournament hole, by hole, shot by shot, but dismissed that idea as half-crazy. I tried to relax and watch a little television. I could not decide what to eat or how much. Looking back, I realized how helpful it could have been to have a coach there with me at Augusta on Sunday.

All the big guns out there, Davis, Nick Faldo, Steve Elkington, Greg Norman, they had their coaches with them. I had no coaches. Every day I would go to the driving range and try to find a new feel. But that Sunday, I had too much time on my hands and could not get a good feeling about even a schedule for spending the time prior to teeing off. Finally, I talked through a time-table with my Dad, Gary Pasquinelli and David Whitt in the kitchen. I ended up still arriving at the golf course a little too early for my liking. As the tee time approached for my final pairing with Ben Crenshaw, however, time sped up to light speed. It seemed like my caddy, Chris Mazziotti, and I were rushing around playing catch-up just to arrive on the first tee box in time.

Sunday Had a Weird Feel From the Beginning

The nerves were working away in earnest when I heard my name announced with Ben's for the day's final pairing. Maybe it was the fact that I was never comfortable with my time-table that day or the sheer enormity of the situation I found myself in. Of course I wanted to win. The nerves settled down after I hit a great drive on number one. But all day long I had a deer-in-the-headlights feeling. Then, during the tournament I began to pay undue attention to my playing partner. A multitude of facts ganged up on me after I made bogeys on number two and number three. Try as might, I never shook the feeling of unease, and I never attained the feeling of being on cruise-control like I had the day before where the golf was coming so easily for me. I had put the brakes on my creative awareness.

18 Birdies Over 3 Days, With None on Sunday

It turned out that Jim Nantz was right on the money once again very early in the telecast on Sunday, April 9, 1995:

> "For the fortieth year, as so exquisitely chronicled earlier [Walter Cronkite had done a terrific historical piece about the Masters, CBS television and of course, Arnold Palmer and Jack Nicklaus to open the show] we want to welcome you to CBS Sports coverage of the Masters. Where by day's end one man will be awarded the cherished green jacket. Ben Crenshaw climbed the eighteenth fairway in tears in victory in 1984. It would be an equally emotional win for Crenshaw today, just seven days after his mentor and dear friend Harvey Penick passed away at age 90. Crenshaw was a pallbearer on Wednesday and has dedicated his play this week to Mr. Penick. And Crenshaw now shares the lead with Jay Haas."

Ben Crenshaw not only won the golf tournament, his 19 birdies were the most over the four days. I made 18 birdies through 54 holes, the most in the field. So when I am recounting my list of "not many people have ever . . . co-led the Masters after three rounds, I can add: ". . . won the birdie barrage after 54 holes" and ". . . were in the last Masters field without Tiger Woods as a professional entry." No list of accomplishments, no matter how significant or unique, will ever stack up against what it would have meant to have made enough birdies to have won the golf tournament. The way I started out on Sunday, I needed to make six or seven birdies to have a chance. By the time I stood on the thirteenth tee, I needed to run the table to tie Ben Crenshaw. Believe it or not, even then, I still thought I had a chance. My only thought on the tee at thirteen was to bust a drive and put myself in position to make an eagle or at least two-putt for birdie to get things going.

Watching Ben Win and Wishing

At pages 64 and 65 of Augusta's official publication, there is a photograph of Ben hitting his tee shot at eighteen. I am in the right corner of the photo, watching Ben. I look at the photo now and remember what was going through my mind then as though it were yesterday: A fervent wish-pounding like a migraine headache—that I was swinging away with a two shot lead instead of Ben.

To this day, I still refer to the 1995 Masters as the most exciting week of my career. Unfortunately, the 1995 Masters is not the year Henninger won. But on that Sunday, if there was an individual I was pulling for to win besides myself, it would be Ben Crenshaw. Standing on the first tee in the final group was nerve-wracking to say the least. Did I think I was going to win the golf tournament? Of course. After the first two tee shots that Ben hit, I would have given him slim hope. No way. But the karma was definitely on his side. Energy and spirit play an important role in life. I expect with the passing of Harvey Penick, Ben approached the day, no matter what the outcome, with great resolve. Often times, just putting things in the right perspective can do wonders for the smoothness of one's putting stroke and put wonderful tempo in one's golf swing. Ben had both. He negotiated

Augusta that day with brilliance. It was as if there was an extra component out there that allowed him to achieve so much more than the rest of the field. He gave up control completely and allowed his great talent to flourish. Call it what you want, but he allowed Superman to fly. Why then? Well, maybe there are supernatural forces that none of us can explain. I am sure that Ben cannot explain. All I know is I witnessed a special day on the golf course and spent the day with a special guy.

I was asked what was exchanged on the final green after Ben Crenshaw made his final putt. I was thinking to myself "what would it be like to be walking off this green having won the Masters?" And then we embraced and I could not have been any happier for Ben. He has always set the standard for what professional golf is all about. Integrity, class, honor and fantastic charisma. I hold the highest regard for the man. The memory of Augusta in 1995 will continue to thrive in my brain's archive of golfing events. But primarily it lives on because of the people I was able to share it with that week. My family and friends were my divine intervention, as was Harvey Penick for Ben.

I have been asked several other questions about my experience at the 1995 Masters Tournament:

The most memorable moment? The sixteenth green on Saturday and making the long putt. It is the photograph of me there pumping my fist, that I chose for the cover of this book.

The hardest part of the third round on Saturday? Had to be the tee shot on number one. Just the butterflies and the need to get out on the golf course and get comfortable. I remember, though, that I busted that one right down the middle of number one. In fact, I drove it perfectly all day.

Davis Love, III and others were still using persimmon woods. Was I surprised that I could hit the ball with those guys? No. Even though I was small in stature, I never looked in the mirror and saw a small person. I always felt like I was six feet tall even though I am five-eight and I always felt I could hit it up with anybody, *at that time.* But, golf club and golf ball technology have changed everything. That is why Augusta National has been lengthened many times since 1995. If they were playing the golf course today at the same length I played it in 1995, it would be absolutely ridiculous for some of these guys like Davis and Tiger, and Fred Couples and Greg Norman the way they hit it now with the new technology. But again, it was so enjoyable back then, because it allowed all players to participate at that level, the Corey Pavins, the Brian Henningers.

What was it like to see your name atop the leader board with all of those great players? It was fun. Greg Norman is the best driver of the golf ball I have ever played with. He hits it *so* straight. Fred Couples is the most physically gifted player I have ever played with. Steve Elkington has the most beautiful golf swing to watch. I also played golf with Payne Stewart before his tragic, untimely death. He had the greatest tempo. He was like a ballerina with a golf club in his hands. It seemed like nobody else in the world could swing a wedge like Payne Stewart because he had that beautiful pace, back and through. That year, Jay Haas played well, and I was fortunate to play a practice round with Larry Mize and I watched Bernhard Langer and of course, Fuzzy Zoeller play at Augusta. None of those golf swings looked similar like so many do now-a-days with today's contemporary technique. But each golf swing had its own beauty because of the tempo each player manufactured through-out the golf swing.

My biggest regret about Sunday besides not winning? I gave my visor away to a deserving young fan who stopped me and asked me for a souvenir: "Please, Mr. Henninger, I followed you all day and I was really pulling for you to win today!" The boy could not have been more than ten or eleven years old and he could not have been more polite—and persistent! So, I obliged and pulled the visor off of my head and handed it to him. I did so without remembering that my player's identification badge, which is really all they give you when you first check-in at Augusta National, was attached to the visor. Now, a young man in his twenties somewhere has the one memento of the 1995 Masters that I wish I still had.

Did I see Tiger Woods at the 1995 Masters? Sure, it was his first Masters, too. He won the amateur medal as the "nineteen year-old freshman from Stanford." Tiger also shot 293 and finished tied for 41st with Jeff Sluman and Payne Stewart. Remember, 1995 and 1996 were the last years before the "Tiger era" truly began.

The ten years since the 1995 Masters have gone by in a flash. The pictures on my office wall are the most significant reminders. It is about the journey for me, so win or lose, the experience lives on inside of me and I my only hope is I get another shot some day. I am not one to reflect a whole lot. Moving on and enjoying new experiences and adventures is what I try to focus on. The experience at the 1995 Masters makes for good conversation with those who are curious. I am often reminded, especially of the third round, by fans and friends and I never turn down the opportunity to discuss the experience. I do not cross paths with Ben Crenshaw very much any more because of the different priorities we have in life. But when I do, there is definitely something special we share. Walking the fairways together in the final pairing at Augusta in 1995. I host a charity Pro-Am golf tournament at Bandon Dunes in the fall of each year. Bandon Dunes is opening its third golf course this year, Bandon Trails, designed by Ben Crenshaw with Bill Coore. Because of the connection, I am hopeful that perhaps one of the professionals in my Pro-Am field will be Ben Crenshaw, if not this year, some day.

My Tie for Tenth Assured Me of My Second Trip to Augusta National for the 1996 Masters

The only solace in shooting 76 on Sunday and 282 for the golf tournament was it meant that regardless of how I played for the rest of 1995, I would be invited back to Augusta in 1996. Sure, the money is better at Augusta, and the $52,000 I won certainly helped Cathy and me and our two babies, Carlin and Hunter. I sure hope the spirit of Mr. Clifford Roberts does not hear that I was talking about prize money at the Masters. When Mr. Roberts was alive and heading up the Masters Tournament, talking about prize money at the Masters would have been almost as bad as referring to Augusta National as a "country club." Or, after Mr. Roberts passed away, being Seve Ballesteros in 1986 and whining about the lack of invitations to foreign players. Seve finally got his wish and sadly for me, it kept me out of the 2000 Masters.

But I have been fortunate enough to have been in the greatest golf tournament in the world twice. The second time around in 1996, I decided to keep a diary. See whether I am able to get you any closer to the action in the next chapter.

With Cathy and my parents, Wayne and Carolyn, at the Masters

With Cathy and Jack and Barbara Nicklaus at the Compaq Classic

Wayne and Carolyn Henninger at Augusta National

David Whitt swings away at The Fireside Chat

Carlin, Cathy and her Mom, JoAnn Bosworth, at the Augusta rental

Carlin with her Godparents, Gary and Barbara Pasquinelli

With Peter Jacobsen at The Fireside Chat Clinic

With Dick Helmstetter at The Fireside Chat

BRIAN HENNINGER'S
FIRESIDE CHAT
2001

One of Cathy's oil painting trophies

With "Team Callaway" at Sunriver North

BRIAN HENNINGER'S

FIRESIDE CHAT 2003

Callaway® GOLF

*"On behalf of our presenting sponsor Callawy Golf,
please accept these gifts as their thanks for your
support of the event.
Wear the Callaway logo proudly! I do every day!"*

*Best,
Brian*

CHAPTER SIX

My Diary From the 1996 Masters Tournament

After my thoughts about Greg Norman, what follows is the diary I kept on my return trip to the Masters for the 1996 tournament. I was invited back because I finished tied for tenth in 1995.

Sadly, the 1996 Masters will always be remembered the most for Greg Norman's collapse on Sunday, a day he began with a six stroke lead. It should also be remembered that the eventual Champion, Nick Faldo, played great golf that day. To this day, Greg Norman remains the greatest driver of the golf ball that I have ever seen. He is also one fierce competitor, on and off the golf course. There is one story, about his bravado off the golf course at the Fred Meyer Challenge that I would only tell with Greg's permission. And I have not obtained that permission for this book. Suffice it to say, Greg Norman does not back down.

If I were granted three wishes by a genie out of a magic lamp, I would burn two of them on the Masters Tournament. The first, of course, would have me shooting 67 on Sunday, April 9, 1995 and beating Ben Crenshaw and the spirit of Harvey Penick by a stroke. The second would be for Greg Norman to have shot a 67 of his own on Sunday, April 14, 1996, to win the tournament going away. I would spend the last wish on long, healthy lives for the people I care about in this world.

Tuesday, April 9, 1996 at Augusta, Georgia

It is hard to believe I am back here again so soon. At the same time, I could not wait for this week to arrive. I have been looking forward to the 1996 Masters since shortly after the last stroke of my final-round 76 a year ago. Yes, I am able to say it now without wincing (well, almost). I shot 76 on Sunday last year. Although I was tied for the lead after three rounds, I ended up tied for 10th with Fred Couples, eight shots behind the winner, Ben Crenshaw.

Augusta National has not changed much in a year. It is still pretty amazing. The first thing that hits me is the condition of the grass. I still remember stepping out of the clubhouse last year and walking to the practice tee and marveling at that green grass. The must feed it special drugs or something. That grass makes you feel like you cannot miss a shot when you are practicing on it. Those kinds of feelings will get the best of you here, if you let them. Conquering your emotions is a huge part of doing well here, because it is so easy to get caught up.

I never even thought I would be playing at The Masters. I thought I would be a tennis player, not a golfer. I did not start playing golf until I was a senior in high school. When I finally made it to the big Tour, it was very emotional. I had tears in my eyes the first time I drove in the gate at the Hawaiian Open, my first PGA Tour event in 1993. So you can imagine what I must have been feeling driving up Magnolia Lane for the first time last year.

It was pretty overwhelming. All I could say was, "Wow!" There is history all over the place. Even the Par 3 tournament was nerve-wracking. There were about four gazillion people watching, and you turn around and Byron Nelson or Sam Snead is standing there watching, too. And, you have to hit a little 85-yard wedge shot. That's not easy. It is certainly a lot harder than taking a full swing at a 5-iron. But maybe it was easier than I thought, because I never, ever thought I was going to be here.

Last year was just incredible for me after the third round. It was almost like I had already won the golf tournament. I tried to keep things in perspective going into Sunday. It just did not happen for me last year. It was not for a lack of experience. I was playing the course pretty well. In the final round, I just did not hit the shots I had been hitting, and the putts just did not fall in like they had been Thursday through Saturday. It sounds pretty simple saying it that way now, but that is how I have had to look at it.

But last year was last year. I have savored the experience and enjoyed it very much. I have talked about it with just about everybody I know or have met. You see, playing well last year will not help me on the first tee Thursday. This year is going to be a new beginning for me. I am going to be in different places, and different things are going to happen. I must put last year out of my mind, like it never happened. So that all I have is the excitement of playing this year.

I do remember being so terribly nervous on the first tee last year, but that is the feeling I want again this

Thursday. Because even though I started out four-over-par after five holes, I made six birdies and finished two-under for the day. But that is golf. It is a strange, strange game. If you asked most of the players this week how they feel, they would say "great." But most of the guys will not play up to their potential, for a million different reasons.

I just love this golf course. It is so different from anything else that we play on Tour. In fact, no one would probably even consider building a golf course like Augusta National today. It is too severe. Everything you have heard about it is true. The greens are incredible. We are talking 5, 6, 7, 10, or 15 feet of break. Sometimes it is very hard to make yourself play that much break. But believe me, it is there. That is why the players with the best imagination are the ones that usually do the best here. And that is why I think I did so well last year.

It was strange. I had never set foot on the grounds before my practice round last year. But I felt like I had been here before. I am not talking about a Shirley MacLaine thing here. Nothing spooky like that. Maybe it was because I had watched the Masters on television all those years growing up. People asked me if it was hillier than I expected. It was as hilly as I expected it to be. I just felt good when I got here, like I was in a good place. It is the same warm feeling I have this year.

I am the first to admit that my play this year has been pretty bad so far. I am only four-for-eight in playing on the weekends. That is not too good. The frustration came to a head last week in Atlanta. I had just had it by the fifteenth hole on Friday. I bent my putter in half and had to play the last three holes without my putter. That is so not like me. But I just could not take missing any more putts. Golf can be a pretty frustrating game. Somebody better write that down. I am hoping that being back here at Augusta gets me back on the right track.

Because this place is like no other, there are plenty of ways to become distracted. Last Sunday, my family and I drove with a bunch of players and their families in from Atlanta in a big bus. When we arrived at the club, at about 7:30 that night, the transportation office was closed. We were unable to pick up our courtesy cars. Yeah, yeah, I can hear you all crying for us poor Tour players. And to me, it was no big deal. But at any other Tour event, the office would have stayed open late. When they want to turn out the lights and go home at Augusta, they just do it.

You have to order your Masters guest badges well in advance of the tournament. But, you never really know how many you will receive. So you write down your Aunt Millie's name, and then you have to call her and say: "Well Aunt Millie, I am officially inviting you to Augusta, but I don't know if you will receive a ticket." The grapevine says that you are safe ordering around ten tickets, but I have heard some of the guys order more. I would never do that. I have not even ordered ten. I am too scared. Heck, if you get greedy and try to order twelve, you might receive only four. Plus, the tournament badges are not good for the practice rounds. You have to order those separately, and specify which days you want. It can get pretty complicated. And, the Masters is the only event that makes the players pay for their tickets.

The price: $100 each. So, if you are inviting ten people: I'll let you do the math. Despite all that, I would not miss this for the world. If you love golf, this is the most enjoyable place to be in the whole world this week. It is just too great of a place to be even a little up-tight about minor inconveniences or quirks in the process.

At most tournaments, you receive various gifts and hand-outs when you register. Not here at Augusta. You are given only a little pin that identifies you as a participant in the tournament. I wear mine on my visor. This year it is blue. The pin has a number on it, corresponding to the order in which you registered. Last year, I was number 73. This year, it is number 52. A lower number, so maybe that means fewer strokes this year? Hey, I'm not that superstitious, but why take chances? I am back at the same house I rented last year, with mostly the same people. And, for sure there is one outfit you will not see me playing in this year: The plaid pants and white shirt that I wore on Sunday last year. Not enough birdies in that ensemble.

I'm thinking a lot about the golf course right now. That is a lot to think about. The course looks simple enough, with its big wide fairways. But that is part of the mystery and the charm of Augusta National. It will lull you to sleep. And remember, the tee shots are crucial because they set everything up. An illustration comes from my practice round yesterday. I was playing the tenth hole, a big, sweeping downhill dogleg left. If you push your drive a little and miss the hill, you will still be in the fairway, but you will have a much longer second shot. Last year, I hit the tee shot on ten perfect every day.

Yesterday, I pushed my tee shot a little bit, and I had 225 to the front edge. I was riding home with my dad after the round and I said: "I don't care if I duck hook it, but my ball is going to be hooking off the tenth tee."

There is also the wind to contend with, which can be trickier than the greens. Of course, you always want to be putting uphill, but, that is not always possible. When you get right down to it, you just hope you are pulling the right clubs on the approaches. You also hope for patience and not aggressiveness. You can really only afford to be aggressive on some of the par fives.

Another thing I failed to realize until I played here is how hard the front nine is. I was really kind of surprised by how difficult the holes play. The first hole is probably the toughest driving hole on the entire course. There is a bunker that sits in the right-center of the fairway. If the wind is against you, that bunker is really hard to carry. And, after all, it is the first hole at Augusta National, and you are going to be a little nervous to boot.

Small guys like me are not supposed to be able to play Augusta the way I did for three rounds last year. I have always been able to hit the ball a long way, even though I'm only five-feet eight inches tall and weigh 145 pounds. Believe it or not, part of the reason is that I *want* to hit the ball far. By that I mean I am consciously trying to create club-head speed. With guys like Greg Norman, Fred Couples and Ernie Els, it just seems to come naturally.

I have not yet heard what my tee time is for Thursday. But that really does not matter. Who I play with is much more important to me. I am not going to name any names, but you really want to get lucky and play with guys like Davis Love, Fred Couples or Nick Price. You want to play with good guys who are going to play well. As for my picks for this year, I like the guys who putt well. Phil Mickelson and Ben Crenshaw, of course. And I also like David Duval.

For me, the keys at Augusta will always be putting and driving. If you are not putting well this week, you might as well say "Adios." I am going back to the same Ping “Anser” that I used last year. If I have both the driver and the Anser going, I think I am going to have a really good week. Yes, I have struggled the last two weeks. And, I might be the last guy that you think could win this tournament. But right now, I feel good. I'm really looking forward to Thursday.

Thursday, April 11, 1996 at Augusta, Georgia

Today was a microcosm of my year so far. My 76 summed things up perfectly. I hit a lot of good shots and got very little out of them. As you will see, it could have been a lot worse.

I started out feeling good and ready to go. But, it is tough to keep those doubts from creeping into your mind when you have not posted a lot of good scores lately. So, I am carrying a lot of baggage out there with me. Until I put everything together and shoot a really good score, my brain is going to remain cluttered with all that extra baggage. And those feelings affect your patience and how aggressively you play the golf course.

I hit a great drive on number one, a very tough driving hole. It was a little cool this morning, and I was a little nervous. But, I drove it perfect, down the left side. All I had left was 135 yards. I hate to use this as an excuse, but I really feel my caddie, Chris Mazziotti, let me down a little today. I did not feel much wind standing back on the tee. But at that point, I just was not noticing a lot of things. That is where your caddie is supposed to step in and remind you or at least make you aware of the externals, such as the wind.

I pulled my 9-iron out, the club I usually hit from that distance. I made a great swing and I "pured" it--I hit it absolutely perfect. To my surprise, the ball came up five yards short of the green. To make matters worse, the pin was tucked behind a bunker, and I really had no shot. I tried to get it close anyway by hitting a Phil Mickelson flop shot with my L-wedge off a tight lie. I put it in the bunker, and then could not get up-and-down. Just like that, I was off to a double-bogey start.

That is a really crummy way to begin any golf tournament, let alone the Masters. I hit two perfect shots and walk away with Six. Then, my putter failed me miserably through the next three holes.

On number two, I missed a four-footer for birdie. Then, at the third, I missed a ten-footer for birdie. At number four, the difficult par-3, I hit a 200 yard 5-iron that was my best iron shot of the day to fifteen feet but again missed the putt. On a good putting day, I am at least even after the fourth hole in spite of my double bogey start. But not this morning.

On the fifth hole, I hit a poor tee shot but received a good break. I had hooked my drive into the woods but there was a fairly wide opening. I concentrated so much on making it through the opening clean that I hit the recovery shot a little too hard. The ball landed hot in the middle of the green and bounded over, and down a slope. That is an almost automatic bogey at Augusta, and so it was for me.

There I was, three-over-par after five, and I had not really hit any bad shots. So at this point, I am trying very hard to find some positive things to think about. You cannot think of any either, huh? My mind harkened back to 1995. H-m-m-m. I was four over after five holes and I came storming back to make six birdies and shoot 70. And that round set me up for back-to-back 68s on Friday and Saturday. . . . Nope. You just cannot let your mind wander like that. The commentators say we draw on great past experiences, but it really just does not work out that way. You simply have to try to collect yourself and move on to better things.

So, I made another great swing and hit a good shot on number six, the other par-3 on the front side. But, I just missed reaching the top shelf of the green where the pin was located. At Augusta, like everywhere else in the world, close only counts in horse-shoes and hand-grenades. I had a forty footer that I felt good about two-putting for par. I also made a routine par on number seven.

Then, on number eight, I had another problem with Chris, my caddy. The hole is a 535-yard par-5 that kind of bends to the left over the last 80 yards or so. I thought the pin was in the back, on the right side of the green. I hit a good drive, and then cranked a three-wood up towards the green. I hit the three-wood a little left, but I thought I was in fine shape to shoot at a back-right pin. When I got up to my ball, however, I saw that the pin was actually middle-left. From that angle, I did not have much of a chip shot. It turned out that I really wanted to be to the far right side in two, so there would be plenty of green to work with. Standing over the three-wood, I was thinking I could really hit it solid to any position in front of the green and be okay. It was one of those times that my brain locked up. In those instances, I want Chris to step up and say: "Hey, remember, now, you cannot hit it far enough to the right here. Just make sure you do not hit it left." Still, I hit my pitch to twelve feet, but I had to putt over a great big ridge. I three-putted for bogey and my second Six on the front nine. So now I am four-over after eight holes but I have not hit four bad shots. Indeed, I still have not hit really any bad shots at all.

On number nine, I crushed a drive and hit my 9-iron to five feet. My putter let me down again as I missed the birdie putt. I went out in 40 strokes, and as funny or unbelievable as it sounds, I really hit the ball extremely well. The ball striking was such that I could have just as easily been four-under par. Maybe that is not so funny after all. But that is golf. At this point, I am feeling awfully frustrated. Turning in one or two over is one thing, and there are some great birdie opportunities on the back nine. But, four-over at the turn on Thursday at Augusta? I was not happy.

So now we come to number ten. Do you remember what I said on Tuesday about pushing my drive on ten to the right during the practice round? I believe my exact words were: "I don't care if I duck hook it, but my ball is going to be hooking off the 10th tee." Excuse me for a minute while I open up my mouth and insert my foot. Today, it probably should have been a three-wood off the tee. But, I had just shot 40 on the front. So, I felt I had to hit the driver. Of course, I duck-hooked it into the woods. I pitched out sideways, and then hit a fat 9-Iron short of the green that came back at me down the hill. I then proceeded to hit a couple more "at-chas." As in, comin' right back "atcha." My two chips went half-way up the hill and rolled back down to my feet. I finally got the ball to stay on the green and two-putted for 7. A dreaded "other." (You know, par, birdie, bogey, double-bogey and "other.")

How did I feel? Only like my brains were about to pop out of my ears. I was seven-over-par and looking at shooting an 80, or worse. An embarrassment. In front of all my friends and family members. It was the most awful, frustrating feeling in the world. As much as I love to play this golf course, at that point, I would have rather been a spectator.

I could almost hear the whispers in the Gallery: "Gee, there is Brian Henninger. He played so well last year. What happened to him? Oh well, let's go find John Daly." You should never think like that, but sometimes you just cannot help yourself. I call it getting in my own way.

But then some good things finally happened to me. I hit two great shots on number eleven, and made my first birdie of the day—a solid ten-footer. That was a really big lift for me, and it brought peace of mind. I was refocused on the task at hand. On number twelve, the famous par-3, I hit the ball right at the flag. The shot came up a little short and ended up in the front bunker. I almost holed the bunker shot for two, and made a very nice par.

On number thirteen off the tee, all I wanted was to give myself a chance to hit the green in two and maybe make a three. At worst, I wanted a two-putt birdie. My wish came true as I hit my second shot to about twenty feet and two-putted for my second birdie in three holes. So now, I am feeling a whole lot better about myself.

Now I am thinking: "Okay, I have another potential eagle, and great birdie opportunity at number fifteen. And there are other holes back here that I birdied last year. Hey, if we can get to three or four-over par, we are right back in business. Curtis Strange shot 79 the first day in 1985 and came back to almost win the golf tournament." I thought about that more than once today.

I made a routine par on number fourteen. Then, I hit a good drive to set up the go at the fifteenth green in two, but I came off my three-iron and ended up some 70 feet from the hole. That putt was very, very fast, and I barely touched the ball to start it rolling toward the hole. It kept picking up speed and ended up ten feet past, all the way to the fringe. But I made the putt coming back for yet another birdie.

So now I am back to four-over with three holes left to play. If I can birdie one of them, without making a mistake, I will be pretty happy. There are some pretty high scores out there today. I hit a good shot on to the par-3 sixteenth and two-putted for par. Then on seventeen, after just an average drive, I hit a great wedge to five feet and made the putt to reach my goal of three-over-par. On the eighteenth hole, I smashed a drive and only had a 7-Iron left. I hit a decent shot, but not great. I was only about 25 feet away from the hole, but there was a crest between my ball and the cup. I left my first putt about five feet short, and missed the next one for bogey.

So, I shot a four-over 76 with a double bogey and a triple bogey. Take those two big numbers away and make them pars and the whole day would have been a resounding success. But the shot I want back the most, believe it or not, is that 9-iron on the first hole. That set the tone for the whole day right there. It was really tough for me to stand on the second tee at two-over par, after hitting two perfect shots. Remember, if you are able to play the front-side even par, you will probably play well coming down the stretch. But, if you are over par coming into Amen Corner, you will probably not have as good a day. I know I did not have a good day, but I played solid on the back nine with birdies at eleven, thirteen, fifteen and seventeen.

Today illustrates just how hard it is to fight back at this golf course. But, fight back I did. That is what I am taking away from today's round. I had to play aggressively on thirteen and fifteen. While that can be very dangerous, what the heck, maybe that is how I should play them all the time?

Maybe I had my whole attitude backwards. Instead of wanting to settle for a couple of pars on the first few holes, maybe I should have said: "Hey look, we can birdie this first hole. We can birdie every hole out here." I did change my attitude after that birdie on eleven today, and I started looking for more. That is the mind-set you really need. You have to believe that you *will* make good scores out here.

After the round, all my friends and family were waiting for me. I wish I could have just gone right into the clubhouse and sat by myself for a while. That is one of the difficult things about this week. There are a lot of people that you kind of feel accountable to. It starts with the people you invited to come with you. So you have to figure out who is coming to dinner. Are we going out? What about the kids? Plus, you know they all feel bad for you but they may not know how to say it. So there is this awkward silence. In the end, they were all really upbeat and everyone told me how great a comeback I made. That helped a lot because even though your first reaction is to be alone with your thoughts, you need that support. No one else out on the grounds cares as much as the people in your entourage. The old joke is that half of them don't care what your score was, and the other half all wish it was worse.

After lunch, Chris and I went to the range to hit balls. And it was pretty quiet out there. I would have felt a lot better if he had just said that maybe he made some mistakes out there. Just like I did. But he did not, and I will have to talk to him about it sometime before tomorrow's round. This kind of thing is tough, because no matter how close you are to your caddie, he is not you. They have a difficult job, too, and they are not hitting the shots, you are. And, they really never know exactly how you feel. But all I'm asking of Chris is that he *remind* me of a few things. That is his job. It is hard, because when my attitude is bad, I am not very approachable. I tend to become real quiet. Anybody who plays golf knows what I mean. But we will be okay. We will sort it out.

I played with Scotty McCarron, who shot 70, and it was nice that he played well. When you are a rookie, you need some good--dare I say lucky--bounces, and he got some today. He made some good putts too. I am happy for Scott, he is a great guy.

My wife Cathy picked up the kids from day care, and after a quiet ride, we arrived at the rental house and I took a nice, long nap. Now everyone is making plans for dinner, but I am just going to relax and get ready for tomorrow.

I see that Greg Norman shot 63 today. That is a pretty good score, but not a real surprise. This is the perfect place for Greg, because he hits the ball so high. I am not surprised at Phil Mickelson's 65, either. He is such a great putter.

I am still feeling good about my chances. If I shoot two-under or better tomorrow, I will be playing here on the weekend. That is all I want right now. I have to be realistic about things, because I have not been playing that well. I will tell you though, that I am close to being right there again. I can feel it. I hit a lot of great iron shots today. If I can make a few more putts and gather a little more confidence with my driver, it is possible for me to get back in this thing. It could happen.

I'm on the brink of something. Something good has to happen, right? Tomorrow will be a good day for me. I can feel it.

Friday, April 12, 1996 at Augusta, Georgia

In every player's career, there are low points. Even Greg Norman, who is leading the Masters after today's round, has experienced lows. Well, I hope that this is mine. Because right now, I feel lower than I ever have in my three years out here on Tour. I shot a 79 today and I missed the cut. I guess you could say I got my wish. I am going to be a spectator for the rest of this year's Masters Tournament.

It was a perfect morning, absolutely beautiful. I had some doubts because of the way I played yesterday. So I desperately wanted to get off to a comfortable start. That, I managed, with routine pars on the first two holes. The second feels like an easy par-5. I hit a good drive, but I was too far to the left and had to try to run it up through the gap. Looking back on it, that is kind of impossible. Though I was hoping to make birdie, I was happy to settle for par.

The third hole is a short par-4, at 360 yards--just a three-wood and a wedge. But not the way I played it today. I pushed my drive to the right, and the pin was tucked left. My approach shot was blocked by some tall trees. I could either try to fade a wedge around the trees--which is not very easy to do--or go under the trees. I only had about 110 yards left to the hole, so I hit a low 8-iron and tried to run the ball up the hill. It was a feel shot that I just did not hit hard enough. So the ball rolled halfway up the hill and turned and rolled way down below the green.

So now I have the very same shot I messed up yesterday: A Phil Mickelson flop shot from a tight lie. And, I did the exact same thing I did yesterday. I flubbed it up the hill and it back down to me. Then I hit it harder, just over the back edge of the green and three-putted from there. So, just like that, I have gone from four-over to seven-over for the tournament. At this point, I was thinking: "Why? Why did this have to happen to me? I just wanted to get through the first five or six holes settled down. Just make it to the back-side at even par for the day. There, I could make some birdies and have a real chance at making the cut and playing on the weekend." I had figured the cut would be at two-over, which is right where what it ended up. But the triple bogey at the short third hole just took the wind right out of my sails

I walked back to the par-3, fourth hole. I was looking at 217 yards to the pin and I had just made a seven. I thought: "How in the heck do you get excited about hitting this shot?" I am so mad at myself, I can hardly swing the club. I tried to focus on what I was doing, but all the bad stuff that happened to me this year, and over the last few weeks, started creeping in. At this point, every little thing is bothering me. And, I am already thinking about putting out on the eighteenth green and driving out of the parking lot.

So I pushed my four-wood to the right of the fourth green. As soon as I saw where my ball was I realized I might as well have written a bogey down on my card and walked to the next hole. Then I also bogeyed the sixth and the ninth. I was six-over at the turn, ten-over for the tournament. Yuck.

It is times like this that you start thinking about what you have left to play for. It is my fourth year on Tour, and I have had some great things happen to me. At the same time, I am not one of the top thirty players, which is where I want to be. So, what can I do to try and build some confidence for the next tournament? I just decided I was trying too hard to hit shots. So it was back to the basics.

Everything was a real struggle on the back nine. Randy Lein, my coach at USC, always told us we should walk around with our heads held high. And never change your expression. Today, I found myself burying my head. That is until I started looking at the people in the gallery and thinking how much they would give to be in my shoes. If you don't believe me, just check the GolfWeb Masters Poll on what people would pay to play Augusta National. I kept thinking that here are all these people that would give anything to be doing what I am doing, and yet, I am miserable.

I thought about that a lot today. It was not like I was moping around out there throwing clubs or anything. But I just did not look happy. And I had become impersonal, not acknowledging the crowd, and that really bothered me.

Hitting the shots was not the hard part. Putting was the hardest part for me, because it was so tough to focus. The golf tournament was definitely over for me, but if I did not force myself to concentrate, it would have been easy to three-putt every hole. So I birdied the two par-5s on the back-side, made a couple more stupid bogeys and then, finally, the round was over.

I had three-putted four times over the two days. Last year, I don't think I had any over four rounds. When I look back at this year's tournament, I see those three-putts and that I made triple-bogey on two holes, number three and number ten. Both holes should be played with short irons to the green. While they are not exactly birdie holes, you really should not make more than par.

I told you about my problems with Chris, my caddie. Well, we really did not resolve anything out there today, so after the round, I told him that we should be apart for a little while. He took it fine, like he was expecting it. We have been together five or six years, and it just may be time for a switch. A lot of guys change caddies out here. It happens all the time. But, Chris will probably be back on my bag soon. So, I will have someone different next week at the MCI. I don't know who, yet. If you know any good caddies, let me know. Just kidding. I will find somebody. I might have one of my friends carry the bag for one tournament, just to make things a little more fun. Then, I will skip Greensboro and play again in Texas.

Believe it or not, after all that, I am kind of looking forward to next week right now. I had lunch yesterday with Lee Janzen, and he said something I thought was pretty neat: "Did you ever just think of a carnival in your mind?" And I smiled at the thought, and he said: "See, you are smiling! It is a lot better to think about a carnival in your mind than a bunch of guys with guns." It may sound weird, but it made sense to me. Literally, just think about something simple that will put a smile on your face. I have so much clutter in there, I have to clean it out.

So, now the pressure is truly off. I will just hang out with my family and friends, shoot some baskets, relax and watch the rest of the golf tournament on television. There was a lot on my shoulders the last few weeks. I was really looking forward to this whole stretch. But it has been one big nightmare, the entire three weeks. I don't know why, but somehow, between now and next Thursday, things are going be better for me. After all, it is not the end of the world. There were worse scores than mine. A lot of great players played badly, just like I did. Things will only get better.

I'm going to stay here in Augusta at the house I have rented through the weekend. But I will not go to the golf course. At least I will be good at what I am doing, because I have had a lot of practice watching golf on television the last two weekends. See, now I am even able to joke about it. It does help to have all these people close to me around me. They tell me stuff like they still like me, that the next tournament is a new beginning and that I am still a good player. That probably sounds a bit hokey, but, believe me, it makes a difference. It is not like there's been a death in the family, but you need that kind of support at a time like this. I get tired of being the focus of everyone's attention all of the time and having all these expectations to live up to. But in the end, I am really glad they are all here.

And my wife Cathy has been really worried about me, too. We had lunch together and talked about a lot of things, like what I wanted to do. She agreed that maybe a change with Chris would be a good idea. One thing she said that definitely helped was that she wanted me to play for sure next week. She said I am playing fine and I just need to turn my attitude around. I appreciated that.

Now, there is still a golf tournament going on. I think Greg Norman, obviously, is in great shape. There are a lot of holes left, but this course is really made for him. If he does not have some kind of crisis, it may not even be close. The key will be the front nine. If he can play the front in even or one-over for the next two days, you can just forget about it. Because Greg Norman can overpower the back nine at Augusta like no one else. Watch out for David Frost, though. I played with him at the Honda Classic, and he is really hitting it great.

So I may not be playing anymore this week, but I will be an interested spectator over the next couple of days. And I do know a little about what it is like to play here on the weekend as the leader. So let's see what happens.

Saturday, April 13, 1996 at Augusta, Georgia

Yesterday I talked about two things to look for on Saturday. First, how will Greg Norman play the front nine? Second, how will he react to a crisis? He played the front side in one-over par. Not bad. And, he had his crisis today on the twelfth hole, and he handled it pretty darn well indeed. After Greg his tee shot in the water, I said to my dad, who was watching the tournament with me: "If he makes bogey here, that would be really big." And that is just what Mr. Norman did.

I would not say the tournament is over. But something very strange is going to have to happen for Greg not to be wearing the Green Jacket tomorrow afternoon. He is just playing head and shoulders above everyone else right now. And if he does win, I think he goes down as the best golfer of the modern era. And by modern era, I mean the best since Tom Watson dominated our Tour.

It remains possible that he could lose. Anything is possible. But I just don't see how. He is just playing with too much confidence; hitting the ball too well; and putting too well. And, he has to be thinking very well. There is not too much more to this game than that. Greg made some awfully strong putts out there today, but none bigger than the one on twelve.

I was not surprised that no one really made a run at Greg's lead today. It was a tough day to play, with the wind blowing the way it was. The television cameramen showed it perfectly when they used a split-screen of the eleventh hole flag and the twelfth hole flag. Those pins are only about 150 yards apart, but they were never blowing in the same direction. I was surprised about a couple of things. One was David Frost's approach shot on number ten. He flew the green and ended up making a double-bogey. That was a big mistake for him because that is the one place you must not hit it on that hole. Also, Nick Faldo just did not look comfortable out there today. But he remains very, very dangerous.

It truly was an incredible performance when you think about all those putts Greg Norman made. People talk about The Masters being a putting contest over Augusta's severe greens. But, I say: "So what?" "I would like to put some of you people who say that out on that golf course and see the shots you have to hit just to get on the greens and into that putting contest. Maybe then you will appreciate how hard the rest of the golf course is.

I really think a lot is going to be decided on the front nine tomorrow. If Greg shoots even or one-over going out, he is going to be very tough to catch. But there will still be some interesting moments. For example, let's say Greg is ahead by four or five shots coming into either of the par-5s at thirteen or fifteen. Assume he hits a good drive. He will be faced with the choice of going for the green in two or laying up. What will he do? I say he goes for the green. The way he hits the ball—its an easy decision. Of course, he probably will not be aiming for the pins. But I think he has to still play aggressively. That is how he got here.

For me, this Saturday was a relaxing day. I watched the golf tournament on television with my dad, which was a rare occasion and was pretty nice. I am looking forward to seeing what happens tomorrow. And if Greg can win it, I hope he is emotional about it. That would be a great scene. With everything that has happened to him here at Augusta: Larry Mize chipping in during that playoff the year after Greg lost to Jack Nicklaus in 1986 on the last hole. He deserves it. I know there will be a lot of guys pulling for him, and I will be one of them. It will be great for golf if Greg wins.

Sunday, April 14, 1996 at Augusta, Georgia

There are probably a number of people shocked by today's final round, starting with Greg Norman. I am not as shocked as Greg is right now, but I am pretty surprised that he's not wearing the green jacket tonight.

I think the whole key to his day was the ninth hole. Greg busted a drive right down the middle of the fairway and only had a wedge to the green. "Short," is the one place you must not hit your approach on that hole. And that is precisely where he hit it. At the time, Greg was only one-over for the day, three ahead of Nick Faldo. Faldo hit first, and went long and left. But with the pin down the hill in front, all he had to do was blow on his putt and it would roll right down to the hole. Greg tried to get too precise with his wedge, and the ball spun off the front of the green and back down the hill. That was a tough up-and-down from there, and he made bogey. That seemed to be a huge momentum swing right there, when Faldo made par and moved to within two shots.

It was especially big because playing number ten, eleven and twelve becomes a lot harder after you have just played the front side in two-over and made a dumb bogey on number nine. On number ten, Greg missed the green short and left. Another place you just must not be. He had been getting up-and-down almost every time, and you had to feel that sooner or later his luck would run out. And that is what happened for another bogey at number ten. At the eleventh, he three-putted, and his lead was gone to Nick Faldo's string of pars.

That is where the demons entered. We all have them. On that back nine, when Greg lost the lead. He may not admit it, but I will bet you he was starting to think about what he would say if he loses the tournament. Or what the press would write. He is only human, and it happens to all of us. Me, I start thinking things like: "What is my Dad going to say? I'm supposed to be this great up-and-coming player." And those thoughts creep in right in the middle of a round.

It was also after the eleventh hole that I noticed that Greg's swing had tightened up. At the par-3 twelfth, he came out of the shot and pushed the ball to the right. He definitely was not aiming at the pin over there. In fact, you could hear his caddy, Tony, tell Greg to aim it at the bunker. But remember, at this point, he is facing the toughest shot in golf, and playing head-to-head with the best ball-striker in golf.

That was the other problem for Greg today. The man who was chasing him, became the man he was now chasing: Nick Faldo is a machine, or at least he was out there today. He plays better in situations like this because he simply has no fear. Ben Crenshaw said it best when he said that Faldo really knows his own golf swing. That is why he does not have any fear coming down the stretch. He knows he is going to hit solid shots.

I think it was huge for Faldo that he was paired with Norman, because Faldo relishes the head-to-head match-up. If Norman had played with Frank Nobilo or someone else, perhaps the outcome would have been different.

So, after losing his lead at the twelfth hole, Norman had to create something, force the issue, and make something happen. But it just doesn't happen at Augusta when you have to make it so. Patience usually works much better. Under those circumstances, once he lost the lead, Greg never really had a chance to catch Faldo.

So what is it with Greg Norman and major championships? Seven times he has led a major going into the final round, and he is now one-for-seven. Maybe it is just bad luck? He has the greatest mind in golf. He has a solid swing. Perhaps he just cannot rely on it when push comes to shove in the majors. I have heard the theory that Greg just tries to overpower everything. For example, on the eighth hole, the par-5, he was in perfect position after a beautiful drive. Faldo had just laid up. So Norman took a metal wood and just tried to bust it up there. But he pulls it left and was lucky to make par. Very lucky. Again, the only place you must not miss that shot is where he did -- which, by the way, is the same place I missed my shot there on Thursday.

As tournament players, we all respect Greg Norman. And there probably will not be a lot of gloating right now. I know I would give almost anything to be where Greg was out there today, instead of watching it on television. You have to hand it to him, the guy is there at the end almost every time. It is a fickle, fickle game that we play.

There is a thin line between being having a mediocre day on the golf course and having a very good or great day. Even for me, as bad as I played the last three weeks, a shot or two here or there could have made an enormous difference in any of the tournaments I played in, including this one. I could have had three good weeks instead of three bad ones.

Phil Mickelson has to be feeling frustrated right now. Especially with how much talent he has. But I think his time is going to come. Yes, he missed a lot of short putts today to fall out of contention. But believe me, he makes enough of them, and it is hard for me to feel sorry for him. He will have his day.

For now, I am just looking forward to the first round at the MCI this coming Thursday. I am glad this week is over, that the entourage has left, and now it is just my wife and the kids. That is just the way I like it out here. For most of us, it is just a job. But to be successful at it, you must live in a self-indulged world. All we tend to think about when we are out here is ourselves. That is just how it is, and to do well, you have to be living, breathing and thinking Brian Henninger the golfer, all the time. Believe me, that can be trying after a while.

Greg Norman must know all about that. Everyone, including himself, has such high expectations every time he tees it up. I am sure there is not one guy who has ever failed to win a golf tournament that is more disappointed than Greg Norman. On the bright side, he did just finish second in a major tournament. He hit a few bad shots that allowed someone else to perform even better. That is just what happened. Life will go on for Greg Norman, just as it will for me. He will try to turn this into a positive. The fact that he finished second, won all this money, was leading the tournament for three rounds. Just like I will. And you watch. We will both be back.

CHAPTER SEVEN

The Experiences at Augusta Changed My Life

"Hey, Where Are You Going Now Mr. PGA Tour Winner? I'm Going to Augusta National"

Brian Henninger, on what every Tour player always said after winning a Tour event before the rules changed in 2000

If you read this book cover-to-cover, you will find a number of occasions where I refer to an event or occurrence as an: "Almost-never-was." My favorite is the "ball-too-close to the rock" episode at the Yale University Golf Course during Connecticut's Ben Hogan Tour stop recounted in Chapter Two . That one was scary, because it could have killed me. But the point is, a lot of the highs and the lows in a professional tour player's life are the culmination of a number of positive episodes and/or calamities. An awful lot of the time, however, you are blissfully unaware of the significance of what is happening while the events are piling up and weaving their way into the fabric that ultimately becomes something as marvelous as my experience at Augusta in 1995. This point is extremely well illustrated in The Perfect Storm: A True Story of Men Against the Sea by Sebastian Junger (Harper Perenial, 1997), one of my favorite non-golf books. And that compelling story shows how this phenomenon applies with equal force to tragedy, as well as triumph.

My Second PGA Tour Win at Annandale in 1999 But There is No Ticket to Augusta This Time

A painful illustration of the "almost never was" effect played out after my second Tour victory at The Southern Farm Bureau Classic back at Annandale in 1999. I was ecstatic to have won another golf tournament, and the $360,000 first prize money was the most I had ever made at any one tournament. The win also got me into the Mercedes Championships, the first tournament of the next year for all tour winners. But I was extremely disappointed to learn that winning a PGA Tour event no longer came with a ticket to the Masters. The rules were changed for gaining entry into the 2000 Masters. Winning a Tour event was no longer enough. The top 50 in the world ranking points and the top 40 on the prior year's U.S. Tour money list would be invited.

At this juncture in my career, the invitation to the Masters was paramount. It had always been like getting to go to Disneyland for the most valuable player of the Super Bowl. When we won a golf tournament, the guys used to say: "Hey Brian Henninger, where are you going?" And the answer was always: "I'm going to Augusta." That is where every body wants to be. I'll be perfectly truthful, the first time I won in 1994, the prize money was definitely the most important spoil of victory. So, it was actually quite disappointing that I did not get to go this time, and I was sad. But I will not say bad things about the foreign players like Seve and Greg that lobbied for years for more invitations for international players.

And, it wasn't just me. There were several 1999 Tour winners in that predicament. One of them was my good friend Olin Browne who had won at Colonial, one of our premier events on Tour. But that is the pain of letting more internationals play on our Tour. It is also the pain of Greg Norman's vision that the best players in the world should play for the premier titles in the world. Still, I don't think the good people in charge of the Masters Tournament fully appreciate how difficult it is to win a Tour event. I have been right there, at crunch time, at least 18 or 19 times, and I have only won twice. There was also some mistrust of the emerging concepts that governed the world rankings and the weight that was being given to some of the internationals. Today, I am certain that there are many, many international players deserving of their high world rankings. Far more so than five or six seasons ago.

I made the point in 1999 and 2000 that it disappoints me that the U.S. Tour officials did not even make an effort to emphasize the importance of having all Tour winners in the Masters field. Ever since I had been on Tour, winning remained a major goal because it meant you were in the Masters. I said I would hate to see the day when players are more concerned with world ranking points than winning golf tournaments. I questioned why the starting field had to remain so small. If the seven U.S. Tour winners who had not otherwise qualified were included, the field would have still only been 102, which is far below the standard tournament field of 144.

We all make choices. For years I have had great success at the B.C. Open. Sadly, the event has always been staged right across from the British Open. (I still like to call it the "Open Championship," as it is known everywhere in the world but the United States. After all, they *were* first). I have always wanted to make the trip to Scotland or merry old England and try to qualify and play in the oldest major. One year, Peter Jacobsen qualified by winning the Scottish Open the week before. But this is what I mean by choices. The money-winning potential for me at the B.C. Open has always been too tempting to pass up, given my history of success there. Indeed, I nearly got my card back in 2002 and a two-year exemption to boot when I missed catching Spike McRoy, another first time winner, by two strokes.

The B.C. Open (I never have known if it is named after Broome County, New York or Johnny Hart's comic strip) is a true throw-back. It is unique. There is not a lot of entertainment in upstate New York, so we are the entertainment for at least a week. The tournament is played on a neat old golf course, and some of the guys bitch about having to buy their practice balls and pay for their sandwiches in the locker room. But you get that feeling there of what the old Tour used to be like in the days before the "shut up" money came along. It is another opportunity to win a golf tournament and a two-year exemption. It has been an incredible spring board for a lot of guys, as it was for Spike McRoy two years ago. I went out early that day, went scary low, and nearly caught the entire field. My tie for third was my only top-ten finish in 2002 official events. So, you see what I would be giving up to fly over and try to qualify for the

Open Championship in search of world ranking points and a better shot at getting into the Masters? I would rather stay disappointed.

No matter how disappointed I was to miss the 2000 Masters, I soon realized how lucky I had been in 1995 to have the rain-shortened Deposit Guaranty Classic victory get me into the Masters Tournament in the first place. I also understood completely, as I hoisted the Southern Farm Bureau Classic crystal trophy triumphantly, how much I really owed to that wonderful experience at Augusta in 1995. An experience, like finishing second to John Daly at the Bell South in 1994, that had changed my life.

Chris DiMarco, another friend of mine from the Hogan Tour and I battled down the stretch for the title at the 54-hole 1999 Southern Farm Bureau Classic. This was the last official event of the year before the Tour Championship. I had played my best professional golf that year and had been very close to winning on two or three occasions. I was able to do what I said we all try to do every week—try to beat the crap out of our good friends who are competing for the same prize. Even though I came out on top that day, Chris has gone on to achieve great success on the PGA Tour. He was quoted at the 2002 Fred Meyer Challenge as follows: "Losing to Brian was great. It was the day I began to not just believe, but to know that I belonged out here."

"Chris, old buddy, glad to have helped you out."

On the Hogan Tour, we used to call Chris the kid because he was this extremely bright kid, right out of college with a wealth of talent. I was 27 or 28 years old when Chris first came out. He could not putt worth a lick, but he could hit it as good as anybody. Once he discovered the claw putting grip, he was off to the races.

In 2001, Chris tied my 54-hole record for low score after 54 holes by a Masters rookie. In the press room at Augusta, Mark Calcaveccia who was also in contention said that he and Chris were going to go out and "claw it around out there tomorrow and we'll see what happens." Neither Chris nor Mark won the Masters with the claw grip that year—that probably would have been another Masters first.

Chris has had enormous success the last three or four years and built quite a financial empire for himself and his family. When I cross paths with Chris, he is still the same kid from the Hogan Tour. A lot of guys who have success just do not change, despite accumulating large personal wealth from their success on the golf course. Chris is one of those guys. I know Chris holds a special place in his heart for the great state of Oregon. To secure his first PGA Tour card, Chris hit an amazing 2-iron to four feet in horrible weather at the extremely long and severe seventy-second-hole of the Nike Tour Championship (successor to the Hogan Tour, now the Nationwide Tour) when the event was staged at Pumpkin Ridge around 1997 or 1998.

Pumpkin Ridge is the same place Tiger Woods won his third U.S. Amateur championship with a surreal come-from-behind performance down the stretch that was a foreshadowing of the awesome things to come from Tiger. There are people in Portland who were at the golf course that day that still tell me they cannot believe what they saw.

If I saw Chris today, it would be as if we were still back on the Ben Hogan Tour. Those are my true friends. And they are the ones that will call you when you are down and need some encouragement. "Hey Brian. Is there anything I can do for you?"

That week at Annandale was an incredibly emotional week. Not only was I very emotionally high over winning and being able to have my father follow me around the golf course, the PGA Tour lost Payne Stewart that week. We were playing in the Pro-Am on Monday. I was on number seven at Annandale. It was one of those incredible Fall days like we have in Oregon. Warm, no wind, and the leaves on the trees were all turning colors. Back there they have spectacular pear trees that turn these deep, vibrant colors. It was there, on our approach shots to the seventh green, that we received the news of Payne Stewart's ill-fated flight that ended in such tragedy for his and five other families. I think it hit me very hard because I play golf, and golf had just lost one of the game's key people. I was not particularly close to Payne, but it hit me as hard as losing a family member or close friend. The golf tournament was shortened to 54 holes because of one day of rain and in observance of Payne Stewart's memorial service on Sunday. We played the final round on Monday.

Unlike the first time in 1994, I was really very proud of this second Tour victory. It felt like a full four-day Tour event. Really, with all of the emotion and delays, it felt like ten days when it was finally all over. Because of everything that happened that week, I think I reached a greater level of appreciation for what I do for a living there at Annandale. Not many people get to do what I do, and I really recognized that during the trophy presentation. Just afterwards, I whispered to my Dad: "Hey, Dad, I'm going to make over a million dollars this year. I never thought when we started this journey that I would make a million dollars over my entire career."

1996 Q School: Another "Almost Never Was"

Mark Wood became my first golf coach on Tour in late 1996 because my game failed a little bit. Prior to that, I was self-taught, with the notable exception of the excellent guidance of Randy Lein, my golf coach at USC. I had to go back to Q School at the end of that year because my two-year exemption from the Deposit Guaranty Classic win had expired. Mark Wood helped me sharpen my game a great deal. That particular Q School (I have now been through it seven times) was another one of those "almost never was" experiences for me. It is an unbelievable story.

I tied for 35th on the number. Back then, the low 35 and ties received their Tour cards. When I shot 65 on the sixth day of the 2003 Q School, I missed a ten-footer for birdie at the last hole and finished tied for 33rd. But, the rules had changed. Now, only the top 30 and ties received cards, and there were only 32 of them handed out. The Karma I was being forced to pay back was on account of this experience I had in 1996.

We played one less round that year because of the foul weather (that should sound like a familiar refrain by now). I made a breaking hit-it-and-hope fifty-footer on the last hole on what turned out to be the last day, to finish tied for 35th and receive one of the 37 Tour cards. I did not know for quite a while after I made that mammoth putt that the last round had been washed-out. It was a huge judgment call for the Tour. I remember sitting in this little cafeteria, watching the wind and the rain, knowing I was in on the number. Of course, all of us at T-35 said: "Why not just call it good right now?" But, of course, there were a lot of guys who desperately needed to play that sixth and final round. The Tour cancelled the last day and I won my card back. This time, I held on to my playing privileges for a stretch of five seasons from 1997 through 2001. That fifty-footer on the 90th hole was ultimately my ticket to my second Tour victory at Annandale at the end of the 1999 season and the first year that I would earn more than a million dollars playing golf for a living.

The Fred Meyer Challenge and Victory With Scott McCarron in 2002

They called it "Peter's Party" for the 18 year-run of the Fred Meyer Challenge. There was always a celebrity Pro-Am, and several stars from the film and music industry would attend the Am-Am on Saturday and the Pro-Am on Sunday. Dan Patrick from ESPN radio came out and did his show remotely from the tournament one year. From what I saw, I think he clearly enjoyed himself. His new colleague at ESPN, Colin Cowherd, worked for the sports radio station in Portland and covered a lot of the tournaments before he became famous and moved to Bristol, Connecticut to join the Mother Ship. We miss you, Colin, and you did a lovely interview with DiMarco the last year of the Challenge on the flagging fortunes of Florida Gator football. Stone Phillips, Dennis Farina, Kevin Sorbo, Samuel L. Jackson and Richard Karn all came more than once, as did the lovely Susan Anton, who is now a famous part of my life.

During the Pro-Am clinic and laugh-fest on Sunday, Susan, all six-feet tall of her, was up on stage with me doing a shtick with Peter. She gave me a hug, so I dipped her and gave her a peck on the cheek. The photograph on the front page of the Portland, Oregonian the next day, however, made it look like I was giving Susan more than just a harmless peck on the cheek. As I was getting dressed on Monday night to attend the main dinner dance (Peter's Party went on for four days), I walked into the bathroom in our house and Cathy had taped the newspaper photo to the mirror. I still catch hell for that one. Gee, I wonder if Jan Jacobsen still gives Peter a hard time about the Sports Illustrated Swimsuit Edition. Peter had a huge year in 1995, winning two tournaments on the West coast, and finishing in the top three twice more. He won over a million dollars in prize money, but he was the envy of the entire Tour because the timing of his West coast hot streak landed the article about him in the Swim Suit Edition. Now that one, he has to hold on to forever.

I bring up the party atmosphere of the event at the front end because long before the Senior Tour landed on the marketing concept, Peter was presenting the game's top players to the fans, up close and personal, in a highly relaxed but competitive atmosphere. Portland golf fans often remarked that having the Challenge come to town once a year was a much better deal than having a regular Tour stop. My only regret over the ten or so years I played in the event was that there never seemed to be enough time to meet all the interesting people, like the celebrities and high powered business people that participated. Samuel L. Jackson had the huge crowd at the Sunday clinic spell-bound as he recited the entire pre-assassination soliloquy about sinners and the valley of death by his character in the movie Pulp Fiction. Fortunately, I have had a chance through my chosen profession, to spend some quality time with Sam Jackson and others. One of the most interesting people I met was President George Herbert Walker Bush, who is an avid, avid golfer and a huge fan of the game. Peter's production company has made several video montages of the clinics and the telecasts of several of the Challenges. Some of that stuff is priceless.

But again, I digress. It's on to the real business of the Fred Meyer Challenge, the golf. And did i have a lot of great golf experiences there. The very first day of the first year I played the tournament I teed it up for Lee Janzen and made eight birdies. That was an important day for me, because it showed me I could play well among golf's elite, even if it was in a relaxed, unofficial atmosphere.

Peter Jacobsen always was able to attract the brightest

stars on Tour to play in The Fred Meyer Challenge in Portland, Oregon. The event ran for 18 years and Peter and his company, Peter Jacobsen Productions helped raise more than *ten million dollars* for local charities. The last two fields in 2001 and 2002 were arguably the finest. The only guy I missed seeing those years was Greg Norman, who had participated for many years and won the tournament with Brad Faxon three years in a row from 1995 to 1997. The 2001 field was comprised of the best-ball teams of Arnold Palmer and Peter Jacobsen, Jack Nicklaus and Gary Nicklaus, David Duval and Bob Duval, Tom Lehman and Sergio Garcia, Fuzzy Zoeller and Jean Van de Velde, Billy Andrade and Brad Faxon (the eventual champions, Fax for the fifth time and Billy for the third), Billy Mayfair and Casey Martin, Fred Couples and Phil Mickelson Craig Stadler and Steve Elkington, Stuart Cink and David Toms, defending champions John Cook and Mark O'Meara, and Scott McCarron and me.

Some amazing golf was played that year. In particular, I remember the best-ball 57 that Fuzzy Zoeller and Jean Van de Velde shot on the second day of the tournament. Neither Fuzzy nor the Frenchman could hit the broad side of a barn in the opening round on Monday and they finished well down the pack. I was paired with Fuzzy in a prior Fred Meyer Challenge and I know when things are not going well he will repeatedly say "you must never, ever give up." On Tuesday, both men were each in double figures for birdies or better on the day. The Frenchman, or "Pepe Le Pew," as his American friends on Tour liked to call him, is a great player and a superb putter. He handled the loss at Carnoustie in the 1999 British Open extremely gracefully everywhere he went, including Portland. Jean must have been asked a thousand times, while he played our Tour for two years, why he did not lay up on his second shot to the seventy-second hole at Carnoustie.

I knew the answer as I was watching the drama unfold on television. It is very simple. Jean Van de Velde has that shot. We all have that shot. A long iron to the seventy-second-hole of a golf tournament with a three-shot lead. No big deal. Hit the shot. And he did. He hit it well. He just lost it to the right a little bit. It is what happened when the ball came down to earth that sealed Jean's fate. He was not lucky. Indeed, the Golfing Gods were not even indifferent. At least three things could have happened differently and Jean would have easily won the tournament in regulation. The ball could have stayed in the stands where it first struck. Jean would have been afforded a drop without penalty. Pitch to the green, even three putt, and win by a stroke. Instead, the ball caromed off the bleachers and hit the stone or concrete edge of the burn (stream) into which it ultimately plopped. Instead of bouncing into the water, the ball could have missed the burn altogether and landed in the tall grass (what Steve Elkington lovingly called "the hippie hair" on the Jim Rome Show. Those Rome/Elk interviews are some of the funniest in golf). Hack it out, chip it close and one or two putt, and you still win the tournament. The same result obtains if the ball, after hitting the stone edge of the Burn, careens into the tall grass on either side of the Burn, instead of into the water that Jean so famously tip-toed into barefoot. It should also be remembered that Jean's drop out of the water resulted in a poor lie that caused his first pitch to miss the green. Yet, he overcame all that bad luck and still managed to drain an eight-foot putt to make the play-off with Justin Leonard and Paul Lawrie. That was one of the greatest pressure putts of all time.

Like me, "JV2V" survived coming up short when he had put himself in position to win a major. He played a lot of good golf on our Tour, and we went head-to-head down the stretch at the 2000 Reno-Tahoe Open where Jean finished second and I finished tied for fourth. I enjoy watching him as a commentator for the BBC at the Open Championship. And, he is such a good player, that we will see him atop a leader board somewhere, some day, soon. Just like me.

At the 2002 Fred Meyer Challenge, my playing partner was once again my best friend on Tour, Scott McCarron. Scott and I were playing as partners in our fourth Fred Meyer Challenge in a row. Just like we did each year before, as we teed it up on number one on Monday afternoon, we promised each other we would let Superman fly and win the golf tournament. Scott played out of his head. He was a birdie machine over both days. All I did was make the birdies Scott did not make, when we needed them. I made a clutch 15-footer on Tuesday in the final round at the par-5 sixteenth hole that helped seal the win. I felt very fortunate to contribute at all, because I had cut my right hand on pieces of broken glass in the hotel the night before Tuesday's final round. I was getting ready to go to the big dance that Jake Trout was throwing downtown at the Oregon Convention Center (just a small function for 2,400 of your closest friends). I dropped the candy jar on the coffee table and it shattered.

My first instinct was to grab for the jar as it fell, and as it broke, all I grabbed was a handful of glass shards. The wound did not require stitches, just a couple of butterfly bandages, but my hand was pretty sore the next morning. That was just another one of those "almost never was" episodes.

Whenever Scott and I talk about the Fred Meyer Challenge, we remind each other that we are the champions in perpetuity, because 2002 was the final staging of that great golf tournament.

Bandon Dunes

When Mr. Callaway admonished me against looking like a race-car driver with signs all over my clothes and tour bag, he noted that it was always appropriate to display the logo of my home course. I have displayed the logo of The Oregon Golf Club for the past eight or nine years. I changed golf club affiliations as this book was first going to press. I am so very proud now to be an official friend of the world-class golf facilities at the Oregon coast known as Bandon Dunes, and to display the resort's Puffin logo on my tour bag. There are three golf courses at Bandon, the original Bandon Dunes, also known as the "old course," the stunning Pacific Dunes, opened in 2002, and opening this year, Bandon Trails, designed by Ben Crenshaw and Bill Coore.

Bandon Dunes is the vision of Mike Keiser, a Chicago businessman. At dinner during the 2002 Fireside Chat, in response to a standing ovation from the golfers, Mr. Keizer shrugged his shoulders, held out his hands, smiled and said simply: "Who would have thought?" Indeed. The development was an enormous gamble. But the golf world is extremely lucky for the risk Mr. Keizer took. Everything about the place puts traditional golf first. The accommodations and food service are first class, and the staff is most welcoming and friendly. There is a rumor going around the complex that in Mr. Keizer's last will and testament, there is a stipulation that no residential improvements will ever be built in the sight-lines of the golfers as they play those beautiful golf courses.

Another feature that makes the Bandon Dunes experience so special is that Bandon is a walking course, and players are encouraged to employ one of the many fine caddies on hand. The caddies make the experience that much better, for most of them are full of wonderful stories about the golf course and the people who have had fun there. Among my favorite stories are those about the errant tee shots off number one at the old course. Caused by those first tee jitters no doubt. There is a lighthouse replica sitting atop one of the buildings adjacent to the course. The building is in front of the first tee, but the lighthouse glass is more than a 45-degree angle from the tee boxes and is quite elevated. Anyway, you can just imagine what has happened to the glass, amazingly, more than once, but I will let you see and hear for yourself. Because if you are interested in golf enough to read this book, you owe it to yourself to go play Bandon Dunes at least once in your lifetime.

Golf carts remain available only in special circumstances for those unable to make the walk. Mr. Keizer and his course designers went to great lengths to keep the cart paths away from the fairways, behind the sand hills and hidden among the gorse and heather.

I will let Brandel Chamblee have the final word, as he described Bandon Dunes after he first played the old course in the 2002 Fireside Chat:

> "Why travel all the way to Ireland? This is a lot better than anything in Ireland, and it's a lot closer!"

The Fireside Chat

If you have read this far, you have likely picked up on the fact that I am highly competitive in the pursuit of my dreams and ambitions. Arnold Palmer said it best at the end of his 1973 classic Go for Broke (Simon and Schuster, with William Barry Furlong):

> "It all started a long time ago as a dream that endured—to play the game with an unreachable perfection."

I approach both the game of life and the game of golf seeking Mr. Palmer's unreachable perfection. As a consequence, we sought perfection when some friends of mine helped me put together a charitable foundation to benefit children. We sought perfection when we designed the Brian Henninger Foundation's key fundraiser, a Pro-Am golf tournament that bears my name and that of Callaway Golf as presenting sponsor. The Pro-Am, known as "The Fireside Chat," moved permanently to Bandon Dunes in 2002, the event's third year. Now, with the help of the fabulous people that work at Bandon and the awe-inspiring beauty of the golf courses and their surroundings, we firmly believe we have achieved perfection. We think we put on one of the finest Pro-Amateur events in the World. *Dans le Monde Entier* .

Our official Press Release after our first year holding the golf tournament at Bandon Dunes tells the official story:

"The Brian Henninger Foundation's

FIRESIDE CHAT FOR CHILDRENS CHARITIES

Marks Third Year of Giving Through Golf

With Donations to Sacred Heart, Make-A-Wish Portland and Special Olympics

BANDON DUNES, Oregon. Native Oregonian and PGA Tour Professional Brian Henninger's charitable foundation conducted its third annual "Fireside Chat for Childrens Charities" at the spectacular Bandon Dunes and Pacific Dunes golf courses on the Pacific Ocean on October 12-14, 2002. The annual tournament raised $25,000 for three charities in 2002, bringing the three-year total to more than $86,000. The Sacred Heart Childrens Miracle Network received $15,000, bringing that charity's three-year total to $69,000. The Portland Chapter of Make-A-Wish Foundation received $5,000, raising its total to more than $12,000 and Special Olympics of Oregon received its initial donation of $5,000 in 2002.

The 2002 Fireside Chat was blessed by incredible and memorable surroundings," Henninger said. 'Bandon Dunes was everything I anticipated and very much more; and the golfing gods smiled down on us with outstanding weather. The opportunity to share this experience with the amateurs that graciously give their time and money and with my close friends from the Tour, fulfills my life-long dream of helping the children of our future through the great game of golf.'

Henninger went on: 'It is truly an extraordinary Pro-Am. My good friends from Callaway Golf take personal time to be there every year, and Callaway has supported the event each year through the donation of tee prizes. This year we were also graced by the presence and support of Mike Keizer, the developer of Bandon Dunes. Every year, each of the amateurs have brought something special to the event through their own unique experiences and personalities. I cannot thank them enough. And every year, Guy Justice or Charlie Hoffmeister from Sacred Heart has done a wonderful job of sharing the charitable spirit with the group by showing the event's donations at work during our formal presentation on Sunday evening.'

There are so many people to thank, including Cordy Jensen of Eugene and David Whitt from Texarkana, Texas who have played in the event all three years, and Denny Collis, Denny McNally, Jerry Laing and Dave Swenson, all of Eugene, who have made generous financial contributions to the event even though they were unable to make the time. I am also very grateful for our corporate participants over the years that have included Bill Yavorsky and In Focus, Lou Ressani and Compaq and Mark Suwyn and Louisiana Pacific. I must also thank Peter Jacobsen, Scott McCarron, Brandel Chamblee, Glen Day, Olin Browne, Dudley Hart, Jim Carter and Paul Goydos for making their way to Oregon with us. Last but in no way least, I want to thank Ed Ellis, the highly accomplished tournament director of the Fred Meyer Challenge and CEO of Peter Jacobsen's management company for helping launch the event and giving it the name 'The Fireside Chat.'

I am grateful to my wife Cathy for her support and for her painting of a fireside chat scene that has become the perpetual trophy and the memento that the winners take with them each year. And I thank my parents, Wayne and Carolyn for their support of the event. Finally, I would be remiss if I did not thank The good people at The Oregon Golf Club, Sunriver and Bandon Dunes for their fabulous hospitality and service over the past three years.

In 2003, the 4th Annual Fireside Chat, Presented by Callaway Golf returns to Bandon Dunes and Pacific Dunes on October 11-13. Charities include Sacred Heart, Special Olympics and The Boys and Girls Club of North Bend. The event begins with a welcome reception and dinner on the evening of Saturday, October 11. Sunday begins with an Am-Am golf tournament at Pacific Dunes, followed by a reception and then the Fireside Chat Dinner with the PGA Tour professionals, fresh from the Las Vegas

Open. Monday, October 13 begins with breakfast, followed by a clinic and then the Pro-Am tournament at Bandon Dunes. The event concludes with a luncheon and brief awards ceremony. The $6,000 package includes two nights lodging, meals, two rounds of golf with caddies, one with a PGA pro and tee prizes."

The Fireside Chat has always been a lot of hard work, however, of all the things I have done related to golf, I find this outing the most rewarding and enjoyable. And, believe me, I know that without my magic week at Augusta in 1995, there may never have been a Fireside Chat. My Dad always comes and I usually am able to play at least one round of golf with him over the weekend. One year, Scott McCarron was able to bring his Dad with him to play Bandon Dunes on the Monday Pro-Am day. It was right after Scott's Dad had been able to watch him finish second to Stuart Appelby at the Las Vegas Open. Scott just missed a birdie putt to win outright on the seventy-second hole, and he barely missed the birdie putt to tie on the first play-off hole. One year at Bandon Dunes, even Scott's caddie, Ryan "Rhino" Scott played in the event and shot 73 without having seen the course before. Scott has always played well at Las Vegas. Indeed, the most raucous party we ever had during the Fireside Chat on Sunday night was the very first year of the event in 2000, when Scott had just finished tied for fourth at Las Vegas and made enough money to secure his Tour card for 2001.

That was also back in the day when Peter Jacobsen participated in the event and we were never, ever short on laughs. The second year, we moved the event to Sunriver, which is another fabulous three-course golf complex in beautiful Central Oregon. The North Course at Sunriver has played host to many prestigious amateur and professional golf tournaments. John Daly went head-to-head with Fred Couples at Sunriver in a Shell's Wonderful World of Golf episode. Part of my vision for the Fireside Chat was to show off Oregon's great golf courses to my friends from the Tour and the amateurs that attend from around the country. Having had such great success at Bandon, and given its awe-inspiring beauty, we decided to make Bandon permanently home after the 2002 event.

But I digress. When we were doing the clinic at Sunriver, Peter Jacobsen started doing his famous imitations of various tour players. From Arnold Palmer pulling out chest-hairs and tossing them skyward to check the wind direction, to Peter dumping a large bucket of range balls into his shirt to become Craig "The Walrus" Stadler. I have never seen Dick Helmstetter or Roger Cleveland laugh so hard. I am sure neither Dick nor Roger had ever seen Peter do his shtick. Peter gives some great insight into the impressions he does and how they evolved in Chapter Five of his book Buried Lies: True Tales and Tall Stories from the PGA Tour (with Jack Sheehan, G.P. Putnam's Sons 1993).

Last year, the Pro-Am was staged at the newer Pacific Dunes course, and Kirk Triplett and Scott Simpson blazed their way to a tie and a new course record by firing eleven under-par 61s. Believe me, these are not easy golf courses. We have been blessed at the Sunday dinner by the presence of Mike Keiser, the founder of Bandon Dunes. All of the people who participate in the event have something to offer and I always learn a great deal. For example, the first year we held the event at Bandon in 2002, Dr. Charlie Hoffmeister from the Sacred Heart Hospital in Eugene, Oregon did a presentation on how prior year's donations had benefited the hospital's premature baby unit. Dr. Hoffmeister passed out the tiny diapers they use and tiny plaster handprints taken of a "preemie's" little hand. Later, during the Fireside Chat portion of the program, as we went around the room introducing ourselves, I was both surprised and struck to learn that of the 45 people in the room, 14 of them had their lives touched by a premature birth.

One of the reasons we think the Fireside Chat is so special is because we limit the field to eight foursomes. The times we are all together are much more intimate—during meals, at the clinic and the Fireside Chat, or even just hanging around together after each round of golf. Also, the golf does not take all day long, so there is time to relax, socialize, or just sit and stare in amazement at the unparalleled beauty of the Bandon Dunes golf complex. At the fifth staging of the Fireside Chat last year, we wanted to make it memorable, and we even had time to try something way, way out of the box.

We came up with a bright idea during a Foundation board meeting held at Carlsbad, California the February before to plan the fifth anniversary event. Dick Helmstetter had invited me and the Board to have dinner, play some golf, and visit the famous Callaway Golf Test Center. The Test Center has probably had more celebrity guests than the Clinton White House, and I am glad the guys that volunteer their time and work so hard on my event were able to experience it. They met David Ledbetter on the range (now there's a golf instruction manual or two). Kelli Kuehne, the fine LPGA player from Texas was there working hard. Mr. Helmstetter was busy entertaining some members of the Japanese golf press. And there was a young kid from Chicago (wearing a Cubs baseball hat) who was the embodiment of where the game is headed. He was carrying drives over the back fence, *out of* the Test Center. Some 340 yards plus the height of the chain-link fence. One of my board members nearly did not make it home, though, as he walked right in front of the "Iron Byron" robot as it was smashing drives deep down the Test Center range. Thankfully, Kristen, one of the superb "techies" on staff, got his attention and probably saved his life. He said later that the whole Test Center experience had him on sensory over-load, and that it might not have been such a bad last experience on earth.

We came away from that trip with a lot of great ideas to make the three days at Bandon Dunes even better. The bright idea (we thought at the time) was suggested by Mike Galeski, Callaway's Director of Tour Player Relations. Mike said that we should all play Night Golf on Saturday night after the practice round. The Bandon staff made it happen, complete with the glow balls, glow sticks and headlamps. There were only a few minor injuries, but there were a lot of very close calls, and let's just say that I have been part of another unique golf experience that will never happen again. I did manage to make a birdie, in pitch darkness, on the par-5 ninth hole at the old course.

Mr. Helmstetter hosted a dinner for the six of us, complete with Kobi beef and a *grand prix* assortment of wines at the fabulous Pamplemousse Restaurant near Carlsbad. Dick told us a story he had heard recently that will undoubtedly become part of the ever-increasing lore of Bandon Dunes. It seems that a rather famous golfer had decided to go visit the resort and play the golf course with a good friend of his, Tim Neher, the President of Seminole Golf Club in North Palm Beach, Florida. The twosome's tee time was fast approaching as they drove up the lengthy entrance to the resort. They hurried to check-in and went straight into the pro-shop at the main clubhouse and lodge next to the old course. The man behind the counter welcomed them to Bandon Dunes and said "Mr. Neher, that will be $135; and Mr. Palmer, that will be $135 for your green fees today." The golfers looked at each other for a moment, handed the cash over to the counter man, and headed out to meet their caddies and play the old course. Arnold Palmer turned to his friend and said, "Wow, Tim, I believe that is the first time in more than fifty years that I have paid a green fee!"

Mr. Helmstetter told several stories at dinner that night. I think we all did. But he told one that strikes me as a great allegory for all time, if anyone ever writes down the "Aesop's Fables" of golf. Dick told the story of the demise of one his neighbor's dogs. There are still coyotes roaming the hills around Rancho Santa Fe. The dog was a Jack Russell Terrier, who like all Jack Russells, thought he was particularly tough. After all, these dogs were bred for the end of the fox-hunt--to chase the wily fox down the hole and kill it. But on this day, the Jack Russell was no match for the coyote. He ended up on his back, with his guts splayed out all over the driveway. Dick concluded with the moral of the story: "This was truly an example of what happens when an amateur tries to take on a professional."

The amateurs arrive at the Bandon Dunes resort on Thursday or Friday. Many stop at Sand Pines, up the coast in Florence, Oregon, to experience another of Oregon's many golf course jewels. Sand Pines is an incredible links course, about a hundred miles north of Bandon Dunes. There is a great book on Oregon's many golf course treasures. Oregon Golf Graphic Arts Center (1999), was written by Paul Linnman, one of Portland's accomplished radio and television treasures. Paul also wrote a journalistic expose on an exploding whale that blew up at the Oregon coast. There is a great Peter Jacobsen story at the conclusion of the book: Peter was asked by the great Byron Nelson where he hailed from when he first joined the PGA Tour:

> "Portland, Oregon" he responded proudly.
>
> "You can't play the tour from Portland," Byron replied. "It's too far away."
>
> "More than two decades later, after playing professional golf around the world, I was still convinced there is no better place to play golf than Oregon." Jacobsen said. "Oregon golf may mean different things to different golfers—that is the beauty of our game. This book captures its many varieties in enticing detail. As a matter of fact, I'm going to give a copy to Byron Nelson."

The Fireside Chat officially begins with a practice round on Saturday, followed by the welcome reception and dinner. Sunday's golf is known as the Am-Am, where foursomes compete for prizes donated by Callaway Golf. Sunday evening my friends from the tour arrive, most of them by private jet from the Las Vegas Open, courtesy of another of my many benefactors, Gary McLean of Tacoma, Washington. We have a "Fireside Chat" with the amateurs after a superb meal put on by the Bandon Dunes kitchen in the McKenzie Hall dining room above the recently-built Scottish pub. If you stare West out of the McKenzie Hall plate-glass windows as the sun goes down, you will swear you are at Royal Troon or Prestwick on Scotland's West coast. And, as the last blazes of the setting sun give way to the dusk enveloping the undulated fairways, mounds and sand hills covered with gorse and heather, a magical picture is painted right before your very eyes. You can hear the bagpipes calling in the distance, and you know you are at an extraordinary place in the world. If only for a few days.

There is a small auction, and super magnum bottles of fine red wine from Mr. McLean's winery, with the tournament logo etched in the glass, are often the top money-maker for charity. Monday morning, usually brisk, but never rainy (so far, I am keeping my fingers crossed), opens with a clinic by the professionals. The highly informative clinic is followed by the Pro-Am competition for more gifts from Callaway and the prized perpetual trophy—a lithograph of Cathy's oils that she painted especially for the Fireside Chat. For the first four years of the tournament, the painting was of three cowboys sitting by the fire in front of their elk tent. Last year, for the fifth anniversary of the event, Cathy painted the breath-taking sea-scape that is hole number six at Bandon Dunes. She has done a great job, and I hope the winners are proud to display their trophy art. Truly, my goal is to make everything about the event a unique experience. One year, among the tee prizes, was a share for each participant from the 2003 bottling of an entire barrel of a Rex Hill Vineyards, Oregon pinot noir. Many thanks to Paul Hart, the vintner at Rex Hill, for that unique experience.

There is always a lively discussion among the Tour players and the amateurs at the "Chat" portion of the Sunday-night dinner. A controversial topic a few years ago was Annika Sorenstam's outing at Colonial. I was in the field, and I made damn sure that I made the weekend. I told everyone at the dinner that I was a big fan of what Annika did that year. She was only testing herself and trying to make herself a better player. She was not being tested enough on her tour. Having played a few rounds with Annika at Carlsbad, I saw first hand her immense ability to play competitive golf. Another favorite discussion topic of mine has always been to chastise the amateurs for not playing the appropriate tee boxes suited to their individual games. It simply makes the day more enjoyable when they do. We also spend time talking about golf books and instruction manuals. I must have over forty-feet of library shelf space dedicated solely to golf books. One of the best books that everyone should read is <u>The PGA Manual of Golf</u>, The PGA of America (1991) by PGA Master Professional Gary Wiren, Ph.D., who spent some of his younger days as a teaching professional in Eugene, Oregon. One of the more interesting books is The Golf Secrets of the Big Money Pros by Jerry Heard, The Hanford Press (1992). When I first started playing competitive golf, I also read several instruction manuals by Jack Nicklaus, including Play Better Golf series (Simon & Schuster, Inc. 1982). It is always good to go back to the basics.

Dick Helmstetter brought a foursome to the tournament for each of the first three years. For each of the last two years, he has hosted two foursomes. Dick has been the event's number one benefactor. So this year, we are naming a special perpetual trophy after Dick to be given each year to a person or persons who have helped us achieve our primary goal of the endeavor, to give money to children in need. Mr. Helmstetter also has his own foundation for charitable work that he maintains with his wife Janine. Dick's example is the primary reason why I wanted to put my own foundation together. I am very proud to be able to say that over the five years of staging the golf tournament, the Brian Henninger Foundation has raised just over $200,000 for charitable organizations that benefit children. One clear choice for the Dick Helmstetter Award this year will be Gary McLean, who has provided his jet airplane as a ferry service for the Tour professionals and donated those fabulous big bottles of wine. At the 2003 Fireside Chat, one of Gary's super-magnums sold for $5,000 and the other for $3,500. Thank you Scott Ehlan and Dr. Curtis Spencer. The good doctor insisted that the group make his bottle disappear that evening.

While I lend my name to the event, bring my friends from the tour and put in the time along with the guys who help me stage the tournament, I must thank the people who really make the donations to charity possible. The amateurs who now shell out the $7,500 entry fee to play in the event and reach in their pockets at auction time. To Dick Helmstetter and guys like Cordy Jensen and Jim Morse who have been there every year, David Whitt, Nelson Clyde, III, Billy Roberts, Brad Mason, Stuart Cohen, John Hanna and Curtis Spencer, Pat Becker Sr. and Pat Becker, Jr., and Paul Gulick, who have played several times. Thank you very, very much for playing in my golf tournament. Finally, I need to thank Heidi Berkman, our operations manager, and Scott Bisch, who takes superb photographs and puts together an amazing slide show while the event is happening. And many thanks to my Board, Bill Mattecheck, Brent Summers, Rex Lindaman, Rick McCloskey and Ed O'Mara, who wears the title "Tournament Director," which means in part that he has to verify all handicaps. Ed is also a hard worker for the Evans scholar program. There are five Bandon Dunes caddies that currently receive Evans Scholarships to the University of Oregon and Oregon State University. Ed wrote our board's mission statement: "We strive for the uniqueness of the event. The concept of our vision is to share some golf at a world-class facility to support those less fortunate. The Fireside Chat is the culmination of all of the things we as a board of directors believe in." Cheers Ed!

Demand is high for the limited number of amateur spots in the Fireside Chat field. We do not even have to spend a dime on advertising the event any more, as the field is full from returning participants. I am reluctantly considering increasing the field from eight amateur foursomes to nine for 2005. But that is the absolute limit in order to maintain the integrity of the event within my original vision. And, due to the already enormous, ever-growing popularity of Bandon Dunes, it will be very difficult to expand the Fireside Chat in the only way I would ever consider it. That would be to duplicate the event on a different weekend. We have always staged the event right after the Las Vegas tour stop, because the professionals are already on the West coast. Many of the caddies I have talked to confirm what Mr. Keizer has often said, that February is a great month to play the golf courses. The breezes are much warmer on the South coast than anywhere else in Oregon that time of year. And, the Tour is winding its way through California and Arizona in February. We will have to give that idea some serious thought.

CHAPTER EIGHT

I Will Be Back! All the Way Back to Augusta

"Golfer fights to reignite his career. Brian Henninger has no 2005 earning but he's 'still alive'"

Portland Tribune Friday, March 18, 2005

We all experience life's ups and downs. My last two-year exemption ran out after the 2001 season. I have been in my first prolonged slump, searching for answers since the 2003 Q School when I just missed getting my card back. I played pretty well on Tour in 2002, as my status as a past champion enabled me to play in 20 events. I had the near miss at the B.C. Open that year, and that is the year Scott McCarron and I won the last Fred Meyer Challenge. I have been working very hard, and after shooting 66 with a double bogey at the Nationwide Tour stop in New Zealand last month, I am at last beginning to bask in the light at the end of the tunnel.

In difficult times like these, my family and friends are all there for me. But at times, they have a tough time knowing what to say and when to say it. Often, they don't say anything at all. Just like the pregnant silence that pervaded our rental house in Augusta after the conclusion of Sunday's round at the 1995 Masters. Finally, David Whitt or Gary Pasquinelli spoke up and said something like: "You played great golf, Brian, what a fabulous experience. You should be very proud." After the silence was broken, we all had a great time recounting the mostly "ups" of that special week in Georgia. It was then that I realized I had given away my cherished souvenir: My players badge that was pinned to the visor that I gave away to the polite young boy after Sunday's round. Oh well, maybe he will read this and consider sending the pin back to me. You never know.

The other support system I have are the close friendships I have made on tour. We really are a band of brothers out there, and golf is a very special sport. It is just as competitive as the other big-money professional sports. But, golf is the one sport where you congratulate an opponent for a "nice swing," "great putt," or "fine shot." (No, David Fehrety, I didn't say "nice ball!"). And, just the positive energy that transfers from doing those things, whether it is on the golf course or off, usually translates into good golf for both players. So in that sense, I think there is an unwritten rule out there: You do not ever root against someone, even if you don't like them. So, there is an enormous bond among us, but that too is a strange relationship because no matter how good a friend is playing against you, you still want to beat the crap out of him each and every week.

It is also difficult sometimes to see some of your friends doing well while you are not achieving as much as they are. But, there is always a huge support system out there. I spent two full years on the Ben Hogan Tour. There was a bigger fraternity of support there than there is on the big Tour. On the PGA Tour, the money is much bigger, and the corporate world pays much more attention to you. So it becomes less likely that you will be able to forge the kind of bonds we developed on the Hogan Tour. Your time becomes too precious, so you really only end up with a few really close relationships on the big Tour. To this day, I still have the very close friendships I made on the Hogan Tour as we struggled up the ladder together. My friendships with Scott McCarron, Paul Goydos, Brandel Chamblee and Olin Browne, the guys that join me every year at Bandon Dunes for the Fireside Chat in October, were all forged on the Hogan Tour.

Traveling a Long Way to Know I Can Still Go Low

I truly am working very hard to find my way back to the big Tour. I had the near miss at Qualifying School at the end of 2003 when I shot 65 on the last day to miss the top 30 by a single shot over six days. This year I made the trek to Australia and New Zealand to play the two Nationwide Tour events over there. I had book-end very low rounds, but the two in the middle caused me to miss the cut at both tournaments by a single shot. The second day in Kiwi-Land I went scary low, making eight birdies and a double bogey to shoot 66. That is something to build on, to be sure, because I know I still have what it takes to get the job done. Now I just need to get into more tournaments to have a chance to put four good days together and win again.

I am only Half Way Through a Wonderful Career

It occurred to me, during the process of writing this book, that some might view my 1995 Masters experience as a "one-hit-wonder." In borrowing that phrase from the music business, I wonder which is the tougher business to be in, golf or show business. You need talent for both, and you need a lucky break or two along the way. One of my big breaks was a historical fact. In 1995, all you had to do to get into the Masters was win a PGA tour event. When I won again in 1999, that was no longer the case.

I have been a professional golfer for over fifteen years, now. In two of those years, I made more than a million dollars in combined earnings from official prize money, unofficial events, outings and sponsorship money. I won three times in one year on the Hogan Tour, including my second time out in 1993 when I was dead-broke and had to have a win. In my first ten full seasons on the big Tour, I won two PGA Tour events, had six top-three finishes, and finished in the top ten seventeen times. I am currently 173rd on the PGA Tour career money list with $3,212,771 in official earnings. I won the last Fred Meyer Challenge with Scott McCarron and my name is on a fantastic Pro-Am that raises a lot of money for children. At age forty-two, I figure I am just now no more than half done with my career as a tournament professional. And, with my competitive nature, you bet I will try to out-do the first half. Here is to believing I will find the magic again, and outshine that unbelievable experience at Augusta that culminated in the third round on Saturday, April 8, 1995. As the Fuzz-man says: "You must never, ever give up." This book is just about the first half of the journey and I look forward to writing about the other half in fifteen years or so.

Be the Best Pro-Am Partner You Can Be

I really have taken Peter Jacobsen's advice to heart. I try to be the best Pro-Am partner I can be. As husband to Cathy. As father to Carlin, Hunter and Mia. As Wayne and Carolyn Henninger's son and John and Celeste's brother. To the extraordinary friends I have made on the journey, both inside and outside the ropes. And, to complete the metaphor, to the hundreds of amateur players that have paid significant sums of money to be paired with me for four or five hours out of their lives. We all have a great deal to offer. We just need to give as much as we take.

Brian H. Henninger
Wilsonville, Oregon
March 23, 2005